Encounter with a New World

Encounter with a New World

A Reading and Writing Text for Speakers of English as a Second Language

Doris Fassler

LaGuardia Community College

Nancy Duke S. Lay

The City College of New York

PRENTICE-HALL, INC. Englewood Cliffs, N.J. 07632

Library of Congress Cataloging in Publication Data

FASSLER, DORIS.
    Encounter with a New World.

Includes index.
    1. English language—Text-books for foreigners.
2. Readers—United States.   3. United States—Emigra-
tion and immigration—Biography.   I. Lay, Nancy Duke S.,
(date)   joint author.   II. Title.
PE1128.F27   428'.6'4   79-4068
ISBN   0-13-274910-6

Printed in the United States of America

10   9   8   7   6   5   4   3

Editorial/production supervision by Ruth Anderson
Interior design by Emily Dobson
Cover design by Suzanne Behnke
Manufacturing buyer: Harry Baisley

PRENTICE-HALL INTERNATIONAL, INC., *London*
PRENTICE-HALL OF AUSTRALIA PTY. LIMITED, *Sydney*
PRENTICE-HALL OF CANADA, LTD., *Toronto*
PRENTICE-HALL OF INDIA PRIVATE LIMITED, *New Delhi*
PRENTICE-HALL OF JAPAN, INC., *Tokyo*
PRENTICE-HALL OF SOUTHEAST ASIA PTE. LTD., *Singapore*
WHITEHALL BOOKS LIMITED, *Wellington, New Zealand*

To my mother, Cheong Choy Ping,
and to my sister, Rosie L. Gonzales,
for teaching me and giving me the
opportunity to experience the new
world.

N. D. L.

To my mother, Elizabeth Bond,
who has always encouraged me; to
Rhoda Haas, whose assistance was
invaluable; and especially to my
husband, Paul Fassler, who made this
book possible.

D. F.

Contents

To the Student

At one time or another, you have probably asked yourself, "Will I ever be able to speak and write English like a native?" This book says loudly and clearly, "Yes, like many others before you, you can gain a mastery of English that is equal to the skill of a native writer."

The reading passages in this book are concrete proof of this statement. They were all written by nonnative speakers of English. They were written by people who came to a new country with little or no knowledge of English—people who had to earn a living, perhaps by fixing shoes, by selling rugs door to door, or by waiting on tables. Like you, these writers had to struggle with the English language while making new lives for themselves. Yet they eventually became published and professional writers of English.

Of course, you have already come a long way toward your goal of proficiency in English, and this book, with its varied language activities, will bring you even closer.

Reading Guidelines

As you read each selection, look for answers to the following questions:

1. What is the main idea of the passage?
   This may be stated at the beginning or it may be understood only after you have read the entire passage.
2. What is the main idea of each paragraph?
   This is usually stated in a topic sentence. However, it may also be implied, that is, not stated directly.
3. What arguments, examples, illustrations, incidents, or other details does the author use to explain and support the main idea?
   You must decide which are major details—those that are essential

to support the author's ideas—and which are minor details—those that help the reader to understand the ideas but are less important.

4. What are the implications of the author's statements?
   The author may want you to understand certain ideas, but not state them directly. You should be able to figure out these implied ideas.

5. Finally, what are the author's conclusions or opinions?
   What meaning or importance has the writer given to the material presented? Are the opinions or conclusions logical? Do you agree with them? If not, what are your conclusions or opinions?

To summarize, look for the following when reading:

1. The main theme of the article.
2. The main idea of each paragraph.
3. Major and minor supporting details.
4. Implications.
5. Conclusions or opinions.

To the Teacher

This text for high-intermediate and advanced students of English as a second language strikes a balance between readers which concentrate on reading skills and grammar-composition texts which are devoted exclusively to the development of writing skills. This is a text that will enable the student to improve all these skills in the course of a semester's work.

The readings are concerned with the experiences of foreigners who have made a new life for themselves in a new country. What makes it unique is that all the selections were written by published and professional writers whose native language was not English. The passages eloquently demonstrate their ability to write proficiently, accurately, often poetically, in their second language.

Thus, our readings will be meaningful to students in two new and important ways. First, they will provide encouragement to those who are now struggling to improve their English, for they are concrete proof that it is indeed possible to gain a mastery of English, even as a second language, that is equal to the skill of a native writer. Second, the selections portray a variety of experiences that mirror and parallel, reinterpret, or contrast with the students' own experiences. This connection between experiences underlies the epigraphs to each chapter which we have chosen from the writing of our own students.

In addition to the reading passage with its glossary, emphasizing context clues, each chapter presents integrative language activities, such as: (1) comprehension and discussion questions for both oral and written practice, (2) a cloze exercise, (3) word form and synonym exercises for vocabulary development, (4) grammar exercises and sentence combining, (5) writing topics with guidelines for different types of essays, and (6) proofreading. This text provides enough material for a complete, one-semester course.

Teaching Guidelines

VOCABULARY

1. *Glossary.* We have glossed only words and phrases whose meaning might not be easily grasped even from a dictionary. Those words whose meaning is clearly indicated in dictionaries have been left to the students to look up. When the dictionary offers a multiplicity of meanings that could be confusing, we have included the word in the glossary. We have also included words whose meaning can be derived from the context.

2. *Context clues.* We would like to provide training and practice in finding the approximate meanings of words directly from the context so that the students can gradually learn to read a passage without looking up every word they do not know. Context clues to meaning may be found in the semantic content of the passage, in the grammatical function of the word in the sentence, or in the morphology of the word itself.

For example, in chapter 1, we have indicated that *regional* has the *-al* adjective suffix, and its base word is *region.* This can lead to a discussion of prefixes, suffixes, and base words or roots. Furthermore, the teacher might discuss how one can determine that *regional* is an adjective from its position preceding the noun *friendship.*

Sometimes, we point out phrases that either convey the opposite meaning of the glossary word or have a similar meaning, such as "a comforting answer" for *consolation.*

3. *Word forms.* Many of our students misuse words that have closely related forms which are nevertheless distinct parts of speech. We have therefore included exercises to distinguish between the different forms. One can teach the following concepts in this exercise:

    a. Parts of speech. Give specific clues to students, such as the fact that nouns follow articles and adjectives precede nouns.

    b. Suffixes and prefixes.

    c. Forms of the verb.

4. *Synonyms.* To help retention of new vocabulary, we have prepared exercises requiring the students to utilize the meanings they have learned from the glossary, from the context clues, or from a dictionary.

COMPREHENSION

1. *Reading guidelines.* The text includes a note to the student on reading guidelines. In addition, at the beginning of each reading passage, we have included a set of questions (entitled *To Think About*) which will guide the student while reading. This thinking while reading will make it much easier for the student to answer the comprehension questions. The teacher

can also use the reading guidelines for class discussions of main ideas, supporting details, implications, and conclusions.

2. *Comprehension questions.* The questions follow the order of presentation of the ideas in the reading passage. They automatically lead the student to read for main ideas, for supporting details, and for implications and conclusions. They are also valuable as a partially controlled writing exercise which allows the student to use many of the phrases and vocabulary in the passage, while permitting latitude in response, particularly to those questions calling for inferences.

3. *Discussion questions.* Since these deal with more far-ranging implications than the comprehension questions, the students will be able to bring their own experiences and insights to bear.

4. *Cloze exercises.* A cloze exercise taken from the reading passage is included in each chapter. This provides still another method of determining the students' comprehension. The importance of the cloze technique is clearly stated by John W. Oller in "Cloze tests of second language proficiency and what they measure" (*Language Learning, 23* (1), June, 1973):

> The information provided in the cloze test allows the student by analysis to synthesize a greater whole. At the same time, the synthesis or projection may become part of the next analysis required to produce a subsequent synthesis. It is interesting to note that the process of taking a cloze test involves more than "passive" reading. By sampling the information that is present, the subject formulates hypotheses, or expectations, about information that is to follow.

In other words, the cloze technique forces the student to think about and concentrate more on the language in order to select the appropriate form to fill a particular blank. This requires more awareness and analysis of the language by the students.

The teacher can use this cloze exercise in several ways. One can go over *all* possible answers for each blank, since there is often more than one grammatically and semantically correct answer for some of the blanks, even if they do not match those in the original passage. Even students' incorrect answers can be valuable for discussion. Write all the answers on the board and go over them one by one, discussing reasons for using one as opposed to another.

Another suggestion is to use this passage to guide students in looking for clues in grammar. For example, only a form of the verb *to be* can occur between *I* and *beginning.* Since the subject is *I,* the list of forms narrows down to *was* and *am* (multiple-word forms are not a possibility because the blanks require only one word each). If the time of the event is in the past, the answer has to be *was.* Cloze passages lend themselves to similar discussion of articles, prepositions, adjectives, adverbs, conjunctions, and in fact, all grammatical functions depending on the passage.

GRAMMAR

1. *Special problems.* Each chapter will focus on a particular grammatical problem that both arises in the reading passage and persists in the writing of advanced students, as we know from our own experience.

2. *Scrambled sentences exercises.* Since word order of complex structures still remains a problem for high-intermediate to advanced students, we include some scrambled sentences. Each exercise will be related to a particular grammar problem. We have included not only single words in the scramble but also phrases, because we feel that students need to see groups of words put together. This will help them not only in their writing, but also in their reading. In subsequent exercises, the complexity of the sentence is increased.

3. *Sentence combining.* Such exercises are particularly useful for students who are just at the stage of developing more complex and interesting sentences. Our exercises at first guide the students to certain combinations but gradually leave them free to develop the skill so that eventually they can work out several different possibilities on their own.

WRITING

1. *Comprehension questions.* As already mentioned, they provide an opportunity for partially controlled writing.

2. *Essay assignments.* Each chapter offers not only a choice of topics, but also a choice of rhetorical modes. Thus, chapter 1 suggests an essay of comparison-contrast, a report of an interview, and a biography. Furthermore, for each writing assignment, we give some instruction about developing compositions, so that by the end of the book, the student will have received a succinct, though comprehensive, course on composition.

3. *Proofreading.* We include proofreading under writing skills because students must be encouraged to regard proofreading and revising as integral steps in the process of writing. Because students' perception of error, especially their own, is extremely poor, regular practice in detecting and correcting mistakes is a necessary part of any writing program. The proofreading passages, taken from essays written by our own students on the same topics, deal with typical errors overlooked in writing by advanced students. Corrected versions of the proofreading passages start on page 255.

SUGGESTIONS FOR GROUP ACTIVITIES

We believe that the use of collaborative groups of students working together is a valuable break from the usual classroom routine. Therefore, we will indicate here those activities in each chapter that are suitable for group work. (Our indications are, of course, only suggestions. The activities can always be conducted in the full class structure.)

1. *Discussion of questions related to the reading.* In a small group in which the instructor is not present as the focus of attention, students learn that they themselves and their fellow students have something worth saying. The small groups also provide better opportunities for speaking English, which is particularly important for ESL students. More students can be talking at any given time than during a classroom discussion. Teachers can control the work done by requiring written reports or essays relating to the discussion or by having the groups report orally to the entire class.

For example, each small group of three to five students can be given a different discussion question or set of related discussion questions, and allowed fifteen to twenty minutes for discussion. Then the class can be reassembled and each group asked to report on their conclusions, with other members of the class being allowed to add their comments.

2. *Grammar exercises.* When students in a small group of no more than five go over grammar exercises, the group inevitably becomes involved in the clarification of grammatical concepts. In cases of disagreement, students will articulate the basis for their choices and will be less intimidated about arguing a point than with a teacher's comment. However, the teacher is always available as a resource to settle questions.

3. *Proofreading.* The proofreading exercises are particularly suited to take advantage of the natural, friendly competitive spirit between the students. Since the number of errors is always indicated, the groups can compete to see which one discovers and corrects them all first.

CHAPTER 1
The Long Trip

I really don't understand human
beings, including myself. For many
months, I had longed for my visa and
permit. However, when I got them, I
hated those documents for I had to
leave all my family and friends. While
I waited in the airport before boarding the plane, what a complicated
feeling I had.

From a Greek student's paper.

READING PASSAGE

About the Author: The son of a Filipino farmer, Carlos Bulosan held onto his faith in American democracy in spite of the discrimination he faced as a Filipino field and cannery worker in California.   His struggles to organize other Filipino workers into unions were interrupted by a different kind of battle, one against tuberculosis, that kept him in a hospital for several years.   The enforced rest allowed him to pursue his reading interests and to work on his poetry.

To Think About: As you read, try to answer the following questions.   (See page xiii for reading guidelines.)

1. How does Bulosan contrast his life in the Philippines with his life a decade later in America?
   (Your answer will be the main idea of the paragraph.)
2. What is Luciano's advice to his brother Carlos?
   (Your answer will be the main idea of the selection.)
3. What are some reasons for his advice?
   (Your answer will be supporting details for the main idea.)
4. What does the author mean when he says, "I was to hear that girl's voice in many ways afterward in the United States.   It became no longer her voice, but an angry chorus shouting: 'Why don't they ship those monkeys back where they came from?' "
   (Your answer will be an implication.)

From
AMERICA IS IN THE HEART: A PERSONAL HISTORY

CARLOS BULOSAN

(A trip to America always involves much more than just the journey itself. It may also mean working to save money for the fare, trying to learn about the country, and eventually saying farewell to loved ones.

In the beginning of the passage Bulosan was working as a cook for an American woman in the Philippines, who later got him a job in a library.)

When our work was done for the day, Dalmacio and I would go to the lake and sit on the grass.

"I will soon go to America," he said one day. "I am trying to learn English so that I will not get lost over there."

"I am planning to go to America in two years," I said. "If I save enough passage money to take me there."

"You don't need money," Dalmacio said. "You could work on the boat. But English is the best weapon. I will teach you if you will do some work for me now and then."

He put a book in my hand and started reading aloud to me.

"Repeat after me," he said. "Don't swallow your words. Blow them out like the Americans."

I repeated after him, uttering* strange words and thinking of America. We were reading the story of a homely man named Abraham Lincoln.

"Who *is* this Abraham Lincoln?" I asked Dalmacio.

"He was a poor boy who became a president of the United States," he said. "He was born in a log cabin and walked miles and miles to borrow a book so that he would know more about his country."

A poor boy became a president of the United States! Deep down in me something was touched, was springing out, demanding to be born, to be given a name. I was fascinated by the story of this boy who was born in a log cabin and became a president of the United States.

I was fortunate to find work in a library and to be close to books. In

Abridged and adapted from *America is in the Heart* by Carlos Bulosan. Reprinted by permission of Harcourt Brace Jovanovich, Inc.

---

uttering   Context clue: This word has the *-ing* suffix and is therefore a verb participle having as an object "strange words."

later years I remembered this opportunity when I read that the American Negro writer Richard Wright had not been allowed to borrow books from his local library because of his color. I was beginning to understand what was going on around me, and the darkness that had covered my present life was lifting. I was emerging* into sunlight, and I was to know, a decade afterward in America, that this light was not too strong for eyes that had known only darkness and gloom.

(Bulosan returned to say good-bye to his family, who were working in the mango fields of San Manuel near their home in Binalonan.)

In the morning I took a *caromata** for San Manuel. The town had not changed. I went directly to the field where mother and I had worked years before. They were all glad to see me, but when I told them that I was leaving for America, they became sad and silent. Then Francisca unwrapped the bit of cloth where she kept her earnings and put the money in my pocket.

"I cannot take your money, Francisca," I said.

She looked at me as though she had something important to say. Then she said: "Take it anyway, brother. When you are in America go to school, and when you come back to Binalonan teach Marcela and me to read. That is all I want from you. We will be working hard with mother while you are gone."

There was a big lump in my throat.* A little girl giving me five pesos so that I could go to school in America! It was her whole year's savings.

I took my father's hand and tried to tell him that it was good-bye. He leaned on his walking stick to keep himself from falling.

"Be sure to come back, son," he said weakly. "When you find it hard and there is no other way, you must come back to Binalonan and stay with us."

"I will come back, Father," I said.

I walked on the footpath that led to the driveway. When I reached the gravel road that finally took me to the highway, I looked back at my family for the last time. I saw my mother in bold outline.* Raising her dark hands, she wept without moving her eyes; without moving her lips, she cried. She put her face in her hands and sobbed loudly between fits of agonized laughter.

I went to Binalonan to say good-bye to Luciano. His wife had just given birth to another baby. I knew that he would have a child every year. I knew that in ten years he would be so burdened with responsibilities that he would want to lie down and die. I was glad that I was free from the life

---

emerging Context clues: "darkness" before and "into sunlight" following.

caromata A horse-drawn carriage.

There was a big lump in my throat I was so upset that I felt as if there was a big lump in my throat so that I could not speak.

in bold outline The shape of the mother's figure stood out sharply against the sky.

he was living. When I had finally settled myself in the bus, I looked down and saw my brother's pitiful eyes.

"Don't come back to Binalonan, Allos!" he said. "Even if you have to steal and kill, don't come back to this damned town. Don't ever come back, please, little brother!" He was running furiously alongside the bus and waving his hands desperately with the importance of what he had to say. "Don't come back as I have done. See what happened to me?" He let my hand go and suddenly stopped running. He was crying and shaking as though a strong wind were bending him from side to side.

(Carlos then went to Manila and stayed for a few days in a boarding house with other people waiting to sail to America.)

In the morning a big truck came to take us to the government detention station. We carried our bundles and suitcases and waited in a wide room. After a while a doctor came and tapped on our chests; then we were taken to our boat. The people began throwing confetti, and suddenly it began to rain. The boat moved slowly out of the harbor.

I stood on the deck and watched the fading shores of Manila. Long afterward I found myself standing in the heavy rain, holding my rattan suitcase and looking toward the disappearing Philippines. I knew that I was going away from everything I had loved and known. I knew that if I ever returned, the first sight of that horizon would be the most beautiful sight in the world. I waved my hat and went into the vestibule* that led to the filthy hold below where the other steerage passengers were waiting for me.

I found the dark hole of the steerage and lay on my bunk for days without food, seasick and lonely. I was restless at night, and many disturbing thoughts came to my mind. Why had I left home? What would I do in America? I looked into the faces of my companions for a comforting answer, but they were as young and bewildered as I, and my only consolation* was their proximity and the familiarity of their dialects. It was not until we had left Japan that I began to feel better.

One day in mid-ocean, I climbed through the narrow passageway to the deck where other steerage passengers were sunning themselves. Most of them were Ilocanos, who were fishermen in the northern coastal regions of Luzon. They were talking easily and eating rice with salted fish with their bare hands, and some of them were walking, barefoot and unconcerned,* in their homemade cotton shorts. The first-class passengers were annoyed, and an official of the boat came down and drove us back into the dark hole below. The small opening at the top of the iron ladder was shut tight, and we did not see the sun again until we had passed Hawaii.

---

vestibule   Context clues: ''the'' indicates a noun; a place that led into the filthy hold.

consolation   Context clue: ''a comforting answer.''

unconcerned   Context clue: This word has the *un*- prefix, meaning not.

But before we anchored at Honolulu an epidemic of meningitis spread throughout the boat and concentrated among the steerage passengers. The Chinese waiters stopped coming into our dining room, because so many of us had been attacked by the disease. They pushed the tin plates under the door of the kitchen and ran back to their rooms, afraid of being contaminated.* Those of us who were hungry enough crawled* miserably on their bellies and reached for their plates.

But somewhere in the room a peasant boy was playing a guitar and another was strumming a mandolin. I lay on my bunk* listening and wishing I could join them. In the far corner of the dining room, crouched around the dining table, five young students were discussing the coming presidential election in the United States. Not far from them was a dying boy from Pangasinan.

One night when I could no longer stand the heat in the closed room, I screamed aloud and woke up most of the steerage passengers. The boy who had been playing the guitar came to my bed with cold water and rubbed my forehead and back with it. I was relieved of my discomfort a little and told him so.

"My name is Marcelo," he said. "I came from San Manuel, Pangasinan."

"San Manuel?" I said. "I used to work there—in the *mongo* fields. I am glad to meet you."

"Go to sleep now," he said. "Call for me if you need my help."

I heard his feet pattering away from me, and I was comforted. It was enough that Marcelo had come from a familiar town. It was a bond that bound us together in our journey. And I was to discover later this same regional* friendship, which developed into tribalism,* obstructed all efforts toward Filipino unity in America.

There were more than two hundred of us in the steerage. A young doctor and an assistant came now and then to check the number of deaths and to examine those about to die. It was only when we reached Hawaii that the epidemic was checked, and we were allowed to go out again. Some of the stronger passengers carried their sick relatives and friends through the narrow hatch and put them in the sunlight.

I was pleasantly sunning myself one afternoon when Marcelo rolled over on his stomach and touched me. I turned and saw a young white girl wearing a brief bathing suit walking toward us with a young man. They stopped some distance away from us; then as though the girl's moral conscience had been provoked, she put her small hand on her mouth and said in a frightened voice:

---

contaminated Context clues: This word has the -ed suffix, which is a past participle ending; afraid of contracting the disease.

crawled Context clue: "on their bellies."

bunk Context clue: "lay on."

regional Context clues: This word has the -al adjective suffix, and its base word is *region*. It describes the noun.

tribalism Context clue: Base word is *tribe*.

"Look at those half-naked savages from the Philippines, Roger! Haven't they any idea of decency?"

"I don't blame them for coming into the sun," the young man said, "I know how it is below."

"Roger!" said the terrified girl. "Don't tell me you have been down in that horrible place? I simply can't believe it!"

The man said something, but they had already turned and the wind carried it away. I was to hear that girl's voice in many ways afterward in the United States. It became no longer her voice, but an angry chorus shouting: *"Why don't they ship those monkeys back where they came from?"*

We arrived in Seattle on a June day. My first sight of the approaching land was an exhilarating experience. Everything seemed native and promising to me. It was like coming home after a long voyage, although as yet I had no home in this city.

Comprehension

These questions are to be answered orally or in writing. Some of them may require more than one sentence for your answer.

1. How did Carlos Bulosan expect to get to America?
2. Why did the story of Abraham Lincoln fascinate him?
3. How does Bulosan contrast his life in the Philippines with his life a decade later in America?
4. Why did Francisca give Carlos five pesos?
5. Why did Carlos have a big lump in his throat?
6. What advice did Carlos' father give him?
7. What was the reaction of Carlos' mother to his leaving?
8. Why did Luciano tell Carlos not to return to Binalonan?
9. During the ocean voyage, how did Carlos feel about his decision to go to America?
10. Were all the steerage passengers as bewildered as Carlos? Who showed a different attitude?
11. How did the steerage passengers get their food during the meningitis epidemic?
12. What was the bond that bound Carlos to Marcelo?
13. What was the result of regional friendships for Filipinos in America?
14. What was the attitude of the first-class passengers toward the steerage passengers?
15. Why was the young white girl afraid of the Filipinos?
16. What does the author mean when he says, "I was to hear that girl's voice in many ways afterward in the United States. It became no longer her voice, but an angry chorus shouting: 'Why don't they ship those monkeys back where they came from?' "

DISCUSSION QUESTIONS

1. When Bulosan heard that a poor boy (Lincoln) became a president of the United States, something deep in him was touched, demanding to be born. What do you think he meant? Why does Bulosan identify so strongly with Lincoln?
2. Do you believe that a poor person can still become president of the United States? Can a poor person today become rich in the United States? Do you think that a black person or a woman could ever become president of the United States? The president of the United States must be a native-born citizen of the United States. Do you believe that this qualification is necessary?

3. Why did the doctor "tap" on the chests of the passengers? Do you think anything could be discovered in this way? What is the passage telling us about the effectiveness of the doctor's examination? What do we learn later which shows exactly how effective it was?

4. Bulosan says that regional friendships developed into tribalism. What does he mean by tribalism? Why would tribalism prevent Filipinos from uniting in America? Are there many of your countrymen in America who came from different parts of your country? Has this regional difference caused problems in the United States? What are the problems?

5. How did the young, white girl on the ship show that her moral conscience was provoked? Is there any real difference between her "brief bathing suit" and the shorts worn by the Filipinos? Why doesn't the girl think that she, too, is "half-naked"?

CLOZE EXERCISE

Fill in each blank with a single (one) word.

I was fortunate to find work _____ a library and to be close _____ books. In later years I remembered _____ opportunity when I read that the _____ Negro writer Richard Wright had not _____ allowed to borrow books from his _____ library because of his color. I _____ beginning to understand what was going _____ around me, and the darkness that _____ covered my present life was lifting. _____ was emerging into sunlight, and I _____ to know, a decade afterward in _____, that this light was not too _____ for eyes that had known only _____ and gloom.

Vocabulary

WORD FORMS

Fill in the blanks with the correct forms of the word given for each group of sentences. You may need the verb (changed where necessary for agreement or tense), participles, a noun (singular or plural), an adjective, or an adverb. For example:

laugh

a. The girls' <u>laughter</u> filled the whole room. (*noun form*)

b. The <u>laughing</u> clown pokes fun at the children. (*participle used as adjective*)

c. One should not <u>laugh</u> when someone else makes a mistake. (*verb form*)

d. I <u>laughed</u> so hard that my sides began to hurt. (*past tense of verb*)

1. **utter**

   a. She is always making important _____ about the state of the world.

   b. He hardly _____ a word during the entire trip.

   c. Just _____ expressions of encouragement is not enough when a friend is deeply troubled.

2. **disturb**

   a. The remarks he made yesterday were very _____.

   b. There was a sign outside his door which said, "Do not _____."

   c. A group of young people created a _____ during the mayor's visit.

3. **annoy**

   a. He is always _____ when he cannot find his pen.

   b. Her husband _____ her every time he screams at her.

   c. Impolite children are _____ but not upsetting to me.

   d. Mosquitoes are a major _____ on warm evenings in the summer.

4. **die**

   a. Old soldiers never _____.

   b. The _____ man was able to tell us who had attacked him.

   c. The _____ of his father has made him so withdrawn that he always stays by himself.

   d. The woman had been _____ for five days when they found her body.

5. **unite**

   a. Everybody should _____ to make the world a better place to live in.

   b. Only a _____ effort of all factions in a party can win an election.

   c. It is important that there is _____ among nations.

6. familiar

a. The incoming freshmen should be ——————————— with the different registration procedures.

b. Foreign students always find it difficult to ——————————— themselves with new customs.

c. Can a travel book provide as much ——————————— with a country as an actual visit?

d. Cinderella is a ——————————— figure in the fairy tales of many cultures.

7. disappear

a. The ——————————— of the child caused some fear in the community.

b. I saw a magician who ——————————— into thin air.

c. After ——————————— into the forest, he was never seen again.

8. emerge

a. The ——————————— of consumer protection groups has affected the quality of many products.

b. As we were talking with him, his son ——————————— from the room.

c. An ——————————— problem for the United States is the financial condition of its cities.

9. responsible

a. College students should be ——————————— for choosing the kind of courses they take.

b. My friend got a raise recently for doing her job ———————————.

c. Parents have the ——————————— of educating their children.

10. detain

a. Her uncle was ——————————— at the immigration office for lack of sufficient papers.

b. The bad weather is ——————————— the arrival of the airplane.

c. Prisoners are often held in a ——————————— house while awaiting trial.

11. desperate

a. In his ——————————— to win the prize, he cheated and was caught.

b. The woman jumped out of the window because she was ———————————.

c. She acted so ——————————— that her friends did not know what to do.

12. **develop**

    a. The boy is well —————————————— for his age.

    b. The athletic field is part of an urban —————————————— project built by the college.

    c. How does one —————————————— the skills of reading and writing?

    d. The still —————————————— nations need help from more affluent countries.

13. **fascinate**

    a. —————————————— by her intelligence, the young man decided to court her.

    b. The way he delivers his speeches —————————————— me.

    c. Astronomy is a —————————————— subject.

    d. The music of my native land will always have a strong —————————————— for me.

14. **miserable**

    a. After he lost his job he became very ——————————————.

    b. The refugees of any war usually live a long time in poverty and ——————————————.

    c. The old man lives so —————————————— in his tiny apartment.

15. **console**

    a. After her father's death, she received many —————————————— letters from friends.

    b. We try to —————————————— each other in times of hardship.

    c. All of his classmates came to express their —————————————— after they heard what had happened to his children.

SYNONYMS

Rewrite each sentence choosing an appropriate synonym from the list below for each underlined word or phrase.

1. deck	6. bewildered	11. filthy
2. contaminated	7. conscience	12. epidemic
3. proximity	8. bond	13. provoked
4. sobbing	9. a decade	14. furiously
5. exhilarating	10. obstruct	15. cabin

1. The writer starts to understand life in America after <u>ten consecutive</u> <u>years</u>.

_____

_____

2. We heard our next-door neighbor <u>weeping</u> last night.

_____

_____

3. The little boy was running <u>angrily</u> after the thief who was stealing his bicycle.

_____

_____

4. He stood on the <u>plank flooring of the ship</u> feeling very sad when he departed for Europe.

_____

_____

5. The passengers were waiting for the conductor in the <u>dirty</u> section of the train.

_____

_____

6. Anyone with a strong <u>sense of what is right or wrong</u> will want to help children who are starving to death.

_____

_____

7. The <u>nearness</u> of my house to my mother's allows us to visit every day.

_____

_____

8. The United States seems to have a <u>widespread outbreak</u> of flu every winter.

_____

_____

9. The Department of Health checks the water system annually because it is afraid the water might be <u>polluted</u>.

_____

_____

10. When foreign students meet people from their own country, they feel a <u>tie</u> between them, which makes them feel more secure.

_____

_____

11. She told me that the first time she visited Europe was an <u>enlivening</u> experience.

_____

_____

12. Every summer they go to Maine and stay in a <u>cottage made of wood</u>.

_____

_____

13. Visitors to New York are often <u>confused</u> by the noise and crowds.

_____

_____

14. The article in the newspaper <u>annoyed</u> me so much that I wrote a letter to the editor.

_____

_____

15. The president's veto can <u>block</u> a law which Congress has passed.

_____

_____

Grammar

THE PASSIVE FORMS OF VERBS

The word *passive* means "not active." (In connection with verbs, do not confuse the word *passive* with the word *past*. You can use the passive in all tenses, as you will see later on.)

The subject of an active verb form is active; that is, the subject is the "agent" or the "doer" of the action.

EXAMPLE

Active: The disease <u>attacked</u> many of the Filipino passengers.

The subject of a passive verb form is not active; that is, the subject is not the agent of the action; it is the "receiver" of the action.

EXAMPLE

Passive: Many of the Filipino passengers <u>were attacked</u> by the disease.

Note that the active agent (the disease) now follows the preposition *by*. The object in the active sentence (the Filipino passengers) has become the subject of the passive sentence. Generally, only verbs that take objects (transitive verbs) can be used in the passive.

Uses of the Passive

The passive is used when:

1. the object or receiver of the action is more important than the agent of the action.

   EXAMPLE

   The speaker was applauded by the audience.

2. the agent of the action is unknown or unimportant.

   EXAMPLE

   Their apartment has been robbed several times.

Forms of the Passive

The passive is a combination of:

a form of <u>to be</u> + the <u>past participle</u>
of the main verb

Passive forms of a verb can be found in almost all tenses. The tense is indicated by using the proper tense of the verb *to be* as the helping verb. The past participle never changes its endings or forms.

In the examples that follow, note that the helping verb(s) show the tense of the entire form.

EXAMPLES

Simple present:	The child is sent to camp every summer.
Present continuous:	The house is being painted today.
Simple past:	He was chosen as the winner by the judges.
Past continuous:	She watched closely while the tire was being changed.
Present perfect:	The truth has never been told.
Past perfect:	The book had been published just before he died.
Future:	The accident will be reported immediately.
Future perfect:	The argument will have been settled before we reach the meeting.
Modals:	These cookies can be baked quickly.
	The patient should be examined by a doctor.
	He would have been insulted if he had heard the remark.

GRAMMAR EXERCISES

A. Rewrite the sentences below by changing the active forms to passive and the passive forms to active. (Remember that the object in an active sentence becomes the subject in the passive.)

EXAMPLE

Turkey permits the production of opium. (active)

The production of opium is permitted by Turkey. (passive)

Active

Passive

1. The police reported the accident.

_____

_____

2. Someone had found the lost dog the day before.

_____

_____

_____

3. Dr. Smith is respected by his patients.

_____

4. The earthquake shook the building.

_____

_____

5. The keeper will feed the animals at 5
P.M.

_____

_____

7. Millions of people have seen the president on T.V.

8. Children should always obey their
parents.

_____

_____

10. The bus takes the children to school
every day.

6. Nothing can be done by the government in this problem.

_____

_____

_____

_____

9. The boys were pulled out of the water
by a man.

_____

_____

B. Correct the passive verb forms in the following sentences.

1. Her watch was lose on Broadway.
2. The story was wrote by an Indian author.
3. The books will sent by the publisher next week.
4. Yesterday the program is heard only on radio, not on TV.
5. Freedom of speech is always suppress in a dictatorship.
6. Eye examinations should give to all children by the age of five.
7. My plants are been watered by a neighbor while I am on vacation.
8. Many people would not have sweep away by the flood if they been
warned earlier.
9. The plane being flew by an experienced pilot when the accident
happened.
10. Should a language taught only by a native speaker?

C. Pick out all the passive verb forms in the reading passage of this chapter.
Explain orally why you believe the author decided to use the passive instead of
the active.

SCRAMBLED SENTENCES

The phrases in each sentence are not arranged in the right word order. Rearrange each group of words to form a meaningful sentence. This exercise will give you some practice in the positioning of relative clauses in a sentence.

1. who became a president of the United States, was, a poor boy, he.

2. the story of this boy, I, who was born in a log cabin, fascinated by, was.

3. what he said, who had Negro slaves, some vicious men, did not like.

4. where she was working, lived, she, near the library.

5. for the Philippines, and died in the war, sailed, where her father had gone, she.

6. to the field, I, where mother and I had worked years before, went directly.

7. unwrapped, where she kept her earnings, Francisca, the bit of cloth.

8. the footpath, I, that led to the driveway, walked on.

9. the gravel road, reached, that finally took me to the highway, I.

_____

_____

SENTENCE COMBINING

Use conjunctions to combine two sentences into one. Many of the examples below will require *so that* or *until,* but you will also find other possibilities.

EXAMPLES

a. I am trying to learn English.
b. I will not get lost in America.

I am trying to learn English <u>so that</u> I will not get lost in America.

a. He worked at many jobs.
b. He earned enough money to buy a ticket.

He worked at many jobs <u>until</u> he earned enough money to buy a ticket.

1a. The people were throwing confetti.
 b. It began to rain.

_____

_____

2a. He walked miles and miles to borrow a book.
 b. He would know more about his country.

_____

_____

3a. I had saved a little money.
 b. It was not enough to pay for my passage.

_____

_____

4a. A little girl gave me five pesos.
 b. I could go to school in America.

_____

_____

5a. He did not go back to his hometown.
 b. He made a name for himself.

_____

_____

6a. I found work in a library.
 b. I could be close to books there.

_____

_____

7a. The boy rubbed my forehead with cold water.
 b. I was relieved of my discomfort.

_____

_____

8a. I stayed in Bagino.
 b. Another year was nearly completed.

_____

_____

9a. I began tutoring the kids in the neighborhood.
 b. They could start school soon.

_____

_____

10a. I was determined to go to America.
 b. My brother was too burdened by responsibilities to go with me.

_____

_____

Writing Assignments

ESSAY TOPICS

1. Compare Bulosan's trip to America and your own; show both similarities and differences.

   Suggested Outline
   A. General statement about whether your trip and your reasons for coming to the United States were the same as Bulosan's or different.
   B. Comparison of reasons for coming to the United States.
   C. Comparison of circumstances. Did you come alone as he did? Did you have farewells with members of your family as he did? Did you have difficulty in obtaining the fare or the necessary permits?
   D. Comparison of the actual trips:
      1. The means of transportation.

2. The difficulties of the trip.
3. The attitudes of American passengers.
    E. Comparison of your feelings about your future in America.

2. Report on an interview with a person who has come to the United States from another country. Do *not* interview your own classmates and friends whose experiences might be similar to yours. Try to choose a person you do not know very well or an older person who came here some time ago. Here are a few suggested questions to ask:

    a. What is your native country?
    b. What made you decide to come to the United States?
    c. What difficulties did you have in getting your visa, etc.?
    d. How did your friends and relatives feel when you left?
    e. Did you have any special adventures during your trip?

3. Write a biography of a poor person who later became a success in life. In your account, concentrate on the person's struggles to improve his or her situation and how she or he managed to succeed. (Your instructor will advise you how to obtain this information in the library.)

PROOFREADING

There are 12 errors in the following passage. Find and correct them. Note: Run-ons (comma splices) each count as one error.

My trip to the United States actually started five years before I arrived in there. In my country, Dominican Republic, we told by our friends that life in the United States would be difficult, we did not know English. My family decided to go to Puerto Rico where Spanish was spoke. However, after four years, we realized that our chances for success was not very great, therefore, we decided to go the United States mainland. First, we studied English for a year to make life more easier when we arrived. When we finally reached New York, the airplane trip seemed very short compare with the five years since we left our own country.

CHAPTER 2
First Impressions

I cannot deny that many things about New York disappointed me at first glance. Whisky bottles and garbage were thrown in the streets. There were pictures of sexy movies on the walls of the subways. Many young boys and girls seemed to be accustomed to the bad habit of smoking, while women looked almost naked in their miniskirts. I had never seen any of these things in my country.

From an Arab student's paper.

READING PASSAGE

About the Author: After coming to St. Louis, Missouri, from a hill village in Macedonia, Stoyan Christowe at first worked in a pail factory and later traveled farther west to Montana, where he joined a work gang building railroad tracks. He saved enough money to attend Valparaiso University, then worked for Western Electric, and eventually became a journalist for such papers as the *Daily News.* Christowe has written four other books in English and has served for twelve years in the General Assembly of the State of Vermont.

To Think About: As you read, try to answer the following questions. (See page xiii for reading guidelines.)

1. Give at least two reasons why Christowe wrote (in the fourth paragraph on page 25) that he was in a "radically different world."
   (Your answer will be minor supporting details.)

2. What is the main idea or thought of the first paragraph on page 26?
   (Your answer will be an implication.)

3. What was Lambo's explanation for the tomato that was thrown at Christowe?
   (Your answer will be the main idea of the dialogue.)

4. What is the main idea, theme, or impression running through the entire reading passage?
   (Your answer will be the main idea of the whole reading passage.)

From
MY AMERICAN PILGRIMAGE

STOYAN CHRISTOWE

The tomato splashed at the nape of my neck. And it was rotten enough. The juice of it felt cold and clammy on my skin. I turned round quickly, and I saw a young face, younger than mine, leering at me from one of the doorless hallways which opened directly onto the sidewalk. My hand itched for* a stone, and it could aim a stone well, but there were no stones here on a city pavement, so instead my hand went to my neck and wiped the mess there.

A man going in the opposite direction stared at me and made me conscious of the invectives* in my own tongue* bursting from my mouth like firecrackers. With clamped jaws and gnashed teeth I tried to suppress the tears. My eyes and nostrils smarted as if they were peppered, and I gulped some of the wrath that threatened to spill out in tears.

Crossing over to the next block, I became aware that my arm was pressing too hard against the lunch package, and I relaxed the pressure lest it should mash up the two fried eggs and the two bananas neatly wrapped in newspapers and tied with string. The eggs, fried on both sides (an American way), were covered by slices of bread to make *san'wiches*. Until I came to America three months ago, I had never eaten eggs, or anything else, flattened like that between slices of bread—white bread.

As I kept walking I was on my guard,* glancing back over my shoulder. I was like a dog that has wandered into a strange neighborhood. The sky was clear and the summer sun was above the flatness across the Mississippi River. There was a haze in the air, and black smoke was rising from the tall chimneys of the barnlike factories that flanked the nearby bank of the great river. The deep, prolonged siren of a steamboat was like a hand pulling at my heartstrings. The stench* of a chemical plant across the street almost stopped my breathing. This was an utterly, radically differ-

From *My American Pilgrimage* by Stoyan Christowe (Boston, 1947). By permission of the author.

---

itched for   Had a strong desire for.

invectives   Context clue: "in my own tongue bursting from my mouth like firecrackers" (explosives).

in my own tongue   In my own language.

on my guard   Watchful.

stench   Context clue: "almost stopped my breathing."

ent world I was in. Even the smells were different. I had never smelled such smells before.

I did not know where this world began and where it ended, where the center of it was, or if there was a center. I could find my way from the house where I lived to the can factory where I worked, and to which I was now going. But where the house and the can factory were in relation to the rest of St. Louis I didn't know, or where St. Louis was in relation to other places in America, or what the other places were. I had no idea where America began and where it ended, what mountains rose athwart it, and what rivers ran across its face. On Sundays, and sometimes in the evening before it got dark, I went down to the bank of the Mississippi to look at the mighty stream. But where it came from and where it went I didn't know.

I walked down the bleak* street, and my heart was full of sadness. The tears still welled* in my eyes, and I did not know whether they were tears of lingering anger or of loneliness and remoteness. The can factory was still five or six blocks away.

Blocks! Already I knew the difference between a "block" and a "street." Ever since I set foot on American soil, I had been asking questions. I was like a person learning a complicated trade, to whom some things have to be explained and some deduced* by himself. And I was learning fast, from what was told me by the older immigrants and from intuition. I would find out about that tomato, too. Already I was beginning to perceive the wherefore of it. But I would ask Lambo just the same. Maybe Lambo had had a like experience.

The tomato still hurt. The rottenness of it hurt. If it had been a stone it would have hurt less. Vaguely, I suspected that it was not just a youngster's prank,* that there was a more profound reason for it. A new wave of anger* surged* through me, and again I had to clench my teeth and tense my face muscles to choke the tears that welled.

I examined my clothing. Everything I had on was American—the blue overalls, the brown shoes that buttoned on the side, with their toes bulging* up like fists, the jacket, the flannel cap, the blue shirt with the breast pockets and attached collar. The overalls, the cap, and shirt were bought *absolutely* new; the shoes and the jacket my father had bought for me "second-hand" from the Jewish stores on Morgan Street. The jacket was

---

bleak Context clue: "my heart was full of sadness."

welled Context clue: This is a verb ending in -ed (subject is "tears"); its base word is the noun *well*.

deduced Context clue: "explained . . . by himself."

prank Context clues: "not just a youngster's"; contrasted with "profound."

wave of anger A very strong feeling that goes through a person like an ocean wave.

surged Context clues: This is a verb ending in -ed (subject is "wave"); "through me" (like a wave).

bulging Context clue: the toes when bulging are "like fists."

not exactly my size, but it *was* American, and "sporty" too. I wore it to work but not while I worked. And look at the words I already knew— "sporty," "stylish," "block," "bluff," "two bits." They were not merely American words I had learned; they were new concepts to me. I knew nothing equivalent in my own language. I was not merely learning a new language, I was learning new things through the language.

At the entrance to the factory, I stopped to wait for my friend, Lambo. Then I saw him. "Say, Lambo, some kid hit me with a tomato."

Lambo grunted in reply. "Yeah, and a rotten one, wasn't it? A rotten one! Right in the neck, eh? But wait till you get an egg, a stinking one."

"Why?"

Both sides of the face grinned, causing a distortion. "Because you're a Dago,* that's why!"

"But we're Macedonians."

"It's all the same. Come on. It's time for the whistle."

Lambo went downstairs to the galvanizing department. I climbed the two flights of stairs to the third floor, where the punching machines stood in rows like people at their morning prayer—with arms folded and heads bowed. An electric bulb in a wire cage hung before every machine.

When the whistle blew, the whole floor went into instant action. I put my foot on the machine's treadle and my right hand started to feed the punch. As long as I kept my foot on the treadle, the punch went up and down automatically, piercing holes in the pieces of metal and bending them so that they looked like ears. As the punch rose the pieces catapulted down a chute into a tub at the back. All I had to do was stand by with foot on the treadle and feed the machine.

In a few days I was as good as the foreman. But the not knowing, not knowing the language, not knowing where I was in St. Louis, and where St. Louis was in America, extended to the work I was doing. There was nothing intricate, or difficult, or important about the work. The machine did the work. I didn't even have to count the pieces the machine punched in an hour, or in a day, or in a week. The machine itself counted them, a meter at the top clicking numbers as the punch fell.

Toward the end of each day a man came along to check the number on the meter. At the end of the first week another man came by and asked my name. He handed me a little envelope with my name written in pencil at the top of it. I opened the envelope, and found eight dollars and three shiny quarters. I took this to be my pay. I had expected someone to come along with a bag of money and hand out to me what was coming to me. Instead, a man carried a tray strapped to his shoulders, and in it the envelopes were neatly arranged.

I liked very much the idea of the envelope. It was the first money I had earned in America, or anywhere, and it was a lot of money. With this much money I could buy a horse or a team of oxen in the Old Country.

Dago   Insulting name for a person of Spanish
or Italian origin.

At the end of another week the same man came by and handed me another envelope. This one contained eleven dollars and some change. I deduced from this—I had to deduce a lot of things—that there was a connection between my pay and the number of pieces I had fed into the machine. And so my knowledge widened by yet another concept: *piecework*. The faster you worked, the more money you earned.

But what I still didn't know was what the ear-shaped metal pieces were called, where they came from, where they went, what eventual use they were put to, why I was punching holes in them.

The ten hours I was yoked to the machine, during which I hardly spoke a word and only heard the whirring of the wheels and the unvaried, rhythmic pounding of the machines, was a suspension of life, a kind of dehumanization.*

In the Old Country work was a part of living. Work and life were inextricably bound up together. There was union between the doer and the thing done. When you pruned the vines you knew why you had to do it, and you could see the sap running from the eye of the slashed vine like tears from a human eye. When you swung the scythe in the meadow you heard the grass sigh as it fell in swaths at your feet. The scythe itself hissed like a snake as it devoured the flowery grass. Whatever you did in the Old Country you understood. And there was an affinity* between the living and work, between the sweat of your brow and the tears of the vine, between your own breath and the earth's exhalation.*

One day Lambo showed me the work he did, galvanizing pails. I looked at one of the pails for several seconds. "Look," I cried to Lambo, "this is what I punch!" I pointed to the ears at the top of the pail where the bale would go. "I punch the holes in them." I said this as if I had made an astonishing discovery.

"Didn't you know that?"

"No! We have pails like these at the flat but I never noticed the ears on them. Just think, Lambo, I do that. I punch the holes. I help make these pails."

"Gimminy, the way you talk for just punching holes! What of it?"

"But now I know what I'm doing. I know why I punch the holes."

"It's still punching holes. What's so wonderful about punching holes?"

"All right, all right, it's nothing."

"Of course it's nothing. It's just holes."

But as I retraced my way between the pillars of pails I could see only the ears and the holes in the ears.

The six o'clock whistle put an end to the whirring of the wheels and axles and the slapping of belts. The machines stood in silent rows. With

---

dehumanization Context clues: "yoked to the machine"; the prefix *de-*, meaning not; base word is *human*.

affinity Context clues: "bound up together"; "union."

exhalation Context clue: similar to "breath."

my jacket over my arm I was walking up Second Street on my way home, but I kept feeding the machine with imaginary bucket ears. My body was tuned to the tempo of the machine, whose metallic clatter kept going in my brain. Crossing over into the block where in the morning I had been struck with the tomato, I began to smart under a fresh wave of anger, and my eyes went to the hallway whence the tomato had come. There was no one there now.

As I turned into Plum Street, where I lived, the block was alive with the black folk who lived in most of the brick houses. Little black bodies in flowery dresses or patchy shirts and trousers played ball in the street or skipped ropes. Older folk sat on the stoops or on benches or wooden boxes against the walls of the houses. Although now I had lived in their midst for three months and had seen them every day, I was still fascinated by their strangeness.

I had always associated black-skinned people with folktales, and this notion was still not entirely dissipated from my mind. The Negroes still seemed to belong to some world wholly unlike this one.

A woman of gigantic proportions was seated on a bench with her skirt about her like a tent. Clinging to her skirt, like an ornament, was a little girl of perhaps five or six, her kinky hair plaited in two braids that stuck out above her ears. As I passed by, a naked little arm, black as ebony, reached out and touched my coat. "Hello, Mistuh Man." The words were not words as such, but sounds made by a musical instrument. With her large, wide-open eyes, perfect white teeth, thick lips, and chocolate skin so smooth it looked lacquered, the little girl seemed unearthly. The mother's black hand stroked the glistening hair.

"What yuh name, Mistuh Man?" the little mouth crooned.

One of the strange things about the Negroes was that they spoke American. Somehow American and these black and brown folk did not go together. I had expected them to speak a language of their own, a black language, perhaps, as unlike American as they were from the Americans. That they were themselves Americans had never occurred to me.

"My name's Alma Jane!" The great eyes blinked shyly and opened wider and brighter. The fleshy arms, naked from the shoulder, rubbed the flowers on the motley cotton dress, and the whole little body swayed coquettishly.*

I felt something dissolving within me and warming my heart. For a brief moment I wanted desperately to kneel down on the sidewalk and stretch out my arms to gather in them this little folktale creature which seemed the most human and alive thing I had seen since I had left my village in the Balkans. "Good-bye, Alma Jane," I waved.

---

coquettishly Context clues: "eyes . . . opened wider"; "body swayed."

Comprehension

These questions are to be answered orally or in writing. Some of them may require more than one sentence for your answer.

1. What happened to the author as he was walking down the street?
2. Who was responsible for the incident?
3. Why did the man going in the opposite direction stare at Christowe?
4. What did Christowe think was unusual about his lunch?
5. In what city did Christowe live?
6. Why did Christowe examine his clothing after the tomato incident?
7. What are two of the new concepts that Christowe learned through the American language?
8. What did Christowe do on his job?
9. How did Christowe realize the meaning of the concept *piecework?*
10. What was the difference between working in America and working in the Old Country?
11. Why did the little black girl seem unearthly to Christowe?
12. What language did Christowe expect black people to speak?
13. Did Christowe think the blacks were the same as other Americans or different? Why?
14. Why did Christowe want to hug the little black girl, Alma Jane?

DISCUSSION QUESTIONS

1. Do you know the geographical relationship of your neighborhood to the rest of your city? Are there rivers running near or through your city? Do they run east or west, or in some other direction? Where do these rivers begin and end? Is all this knowledge important or meaningful to you?
2. Why did Christowe call words like *sporty, stylish, block,* and *bluff* not merely new American words, but new concepts?
3. Why was it the rottenness of the tomato that hurt? Why would it have hurt less if it had been a stone?
4. Nowadays many people talk about the dehumanization of modern life. Christowe refers specifically to his job. In what other ways is modern life dehumanizing?
5. Why does Christowe see only the ears and the holes in the ears? How does this new perception relate to his feeling that his work is dehumanizing?

CLOZE EXERCISE

Fill in each blank with a single (one) word.

The six o'clock whistle put _____ end to the whirring of _____ wheels and axles and the _____ of belts. The machines stood _____ silent rows. With my jacket _____ my arm I was walking _____ Second Street on my way _____, but I kept feeding the _____ with imaginary bucket ears. My _____ was tuned to the tempo _____ the machine, whose metallic clatter _____ going in my brain. Crossing _____ into the block where in _____ morning I had been struck _____ the tomato, I began to _____ under a fresh wave of _____, and my eyes went to _____ hallway whence the tomato had _____. There was no one there _____.

Vocabulary

WORD FORMS

Fill in the blanks with the correct forms of the word given for each group of sentences. You may need the verb (changed where necessary for agreement or tense), participles, a noun (singular or plural), an adjective, or an adverb. For example:

complicate
a. The adoption of a child made their life <u>complicated</u>. (*adjective*)
b. He always <u>complicates</u> his life by trying to do too many things at once. (*verb*)
c. The patient died as a result of <u>complications</u> caused by the operation. (*noun*)

1. **conscious**

a. His remarks made me very _____ of my clothing.

b. The little boy regained _____ immediately after his fall.

c. She tried _____ to keep her temper.

2. **deduce**

a. The policeman's _____ of the murderer's identity solved the case.

b. Students must learn how to _____ implications from what they read.

c. My father often _____ what I am thinking from the expression on my face.

3. **perceive**

   a. Some colors are not easily _____.

   b. He was beginning to _____ what I was trying to explain.

   c. Ms. Jones has a good _____ of shapes and space.

4. **distort**

   a. Elizabeth gave me a _____ picture of her family.

   b. Do you think that wearing makeup is a _____ of nature?

   c. The child is _____ his face by pulling at his lip.

5. **remote**

   a. Your conclusions are not even _____ connected with your facts.

   b. Do you have a _____ control device on your television set?

   c. The _____ of their summer cottage made it difficult for people to visit them.

   d. The Far East seems so _____ to Americans.

6. **rhythm**

   a. In dancing, one has to have a good sense of _____.

   b. One can hear the _____ pounding of machines in a factory.

   c. His body moved _____ in time to the music.

7. **glisten**

   a. The children like to touch their mother's _____ hair.

   b. Early in the morning, the water in the lake seems to _____ as the sun shines on it.

   c. His eyes _____ in the moonlight even though it was quite dark.

9. **dissipate**

   a. The young man has already _____ his entire inheritance.

   b. The _____ of the country's natural resources is a serious problem.

c. One should conserve, not ————————————, one's energy.

10. **dehumanize**

   a. Many technological inventions have ———————————— our daily life.

   b. The use of computers encourages the ———————————— of our society.

   c. War and torture are ———————————— to human beings.

11. **dissolve**

   a. Will sugar ———————————— in cold water?

   b. The ———————————— of large families has caused many psychological problems.

   c. I felt my problems ———————————— as he spoke kindly to me.

12. **intuitive**

   a. The discoveries of great scientists are often the result of ———————————— guesses.

   b. He was learning fast about America from books, from friends, and from

   ————————————.

   c. Whenever he is in a difficult situation, he always acts ————————————.

13. **intricate**

   a. It took us a long time to come to a solution because of the ———————————— of the problem.

   b. The tapestry hanging on the wall is an ———————————— work of art.

   c. Notice how ———————————— the artist has carved this piece of wood.

14. **discontent**

   a. My friends were ———————————— with the summer resort they went to.

   b. The poor have many reasons for ———————————— with their lives.

   c. She worked ———————————— because the job was boring.

15. **imitate**

   a. The suit I saw in the shop window is just an ———————————— of an original design.

   b. Children often ———————————— their parents in whatever they do.

   c. Are actors just ———————————— of real people?

SYNONYMS

Rewrite each sentence choosing an appropriate synonym from the list below for each underlined word or phrase.

1. pranks	6. invectives	11. nape
2. devoured	7. gigantic	12. keg
3. stench	8. linger	13. leering
4. concepts	9. bleak	14. sirens
5. eventually	10. accentuated	15. profound

1. As he turned around, the writer saw a young man looking slyly at him.

_____

_____

2. During the winter time, the streets in the city look cold and dreary.

_____

_____

3. My friend apologized for the curse words he had used in front of the children.

_____

_____

4. The piercing whistles of the fire engines frightened the entire neighborhood.

_____

_____

5. The strong, offensive odor coming from the factories pollutes the air.

_____

_____

6. She felt some pain in the back of her neck.

_____

_____

7. When they travel, they like to remain long in one place.

_____

_____

8. Their wine is stored in a small barrel down in the cellar.

_____

_____

9. Many people all over the world have deep respect for Abraham Lincoln.

_____

_____

10. When the writer first arrived in this country, he learned many new American ideas.

_____

_____

11. The neighborhood children like to play mischievous tricks on strangers.

_____

_____

12. The statue in the plaza looks huge.

_____

_____

13. The hungry child ate the food quickly in large gulps.

_____

_____

14. The English professor who lectured to us emphasized his words with many gestures.

_____

_____

15. When he has spent all his money, he will ultimately have to look for a job.

_____

_____

METAPHORICAL LANGUAGE

Some writers make their writing more alive, colorful, and meaningful by using comparisons that are unusual and that one might not find in ordinary speech. Such a comparison is called a *metaphor*. When the metaphor or comparison is introduced by such words as "like" or "as if," it is also called a *simile*. For example, in the second paragraph on page 25 Christowe mentions that he became "conscious of the invectives in my own tongue bursting from my mouth *like* firecrackers." If he had merely said that he cursed or that he used many invectives, would we have understood as well how he really felt? Instead, we can feel how very angry he was when we realize that his curses were like explosives, like firecrackers that were sharp and made a lot of noise.

Sometimes, the comparison is made directly without using "like." For example, in the third paragraph on page 28 Christowe writes about the "ten hours I was yoked to the machine. . . ." Christowe was not actually tied to the machine, but his language indicates that he felt like an animal—an ox, perhaps, which is often yoked (tied) to carts or other machinery in primitive societies.

Exercise: There are at least ten other examples of metaphorical language in the reading passage. Find them and discuss (in writing or orally) how their use expands the meaning of the sentence.

Grammar

PRESENT PARTICIPIAL PHRASES I

The *-ing* form of any verb (listen*ing*, be*ing*, do*ing*), also known as the present participle, can introduce a group of words to form a participial phrase.

EXAMPLE

<u>crossing</u> over to the next block

However, a participial phrase cannot stand alone, but must be part of a complete sentence in which it modifies or refers to a noun or pronoun (as indicated by arrows below).

EXAMPLES

<u>Crossing over to the next block,</u> I became aware that my arm was pressing too hard against the lunch package.

The child <u>looking out of the window</u> seems to be in a dangerous position.

Everyone noticed him <u>running away from the crowd.</u>

Position and Punctuation of Participial Phrases

A. When a participial phrase refers to a word that is NOT the subject of the sentence, the phrase cannot come before that word but must come *after* it.

EXAMPLES

I saw a young face leering at me. (*Subject:* I)
We heard the news from the man living in the next block. (*Subject:* We)

Punctuation: No commas are necessary when the *-ing* phrase refers to a word that is not a subject.

B. Participial phrases modifying or referring to subjects may appear in various positions:

1. *Before the subject.*

EXAMPLE
Pushing back her black hair, the girl grinned at the foreigner.
(*Subject:* girl)

Punctuation: A comma sets off the phrase from the rest of the sentence.

2. *Following the subject.*
EXAMPLE
A man going in the opposite direction stared at me. (*Subject:* man)

Punctuation: No comma is used with an *identifying* phrase, that is, one that is needed to identify the subject.

EXAMPLE
The heavy snowfall, arriving in mid-winter, did not melt until late spring.
(*Subject:* snowfall)

Punctuation: Commas set off a *nonidentifying* phrase, that is, one that is not needed to identify the subject.

3. *At the end of the sentence.*

EXAMPLE
I was on my guard, glancing back over my shoulder. (*Subject:* I)

Punctuation: A comma usually separates a participial phrase at the end of a sentence when it refers back to the subject, though sometimes it may be omitted.

Do not use position 3 if the sentence is so long that the participial phrase is too far away from the subject to make sense.   For example:

WRONG: The new teacher found that his class was quite enjoyable, expecting the worst.

RIGHT: Expecting the worst, the new teacher found that his class was quite enjoyable.

RIGHT: The new teacher, expecting the worst, found that his class was quite enjoyable.

GRAMMAR EXERCISES

A. Insert the participial phrase into its corresponding sentence so that it modifies the underlined word(s). Write out the new sentence. (When possible, try different positions for the participial phrase.)

Participial Phrase	*Sentence*
1. containing reports on current events	<u>Magazines like Newsweek</u> can be useful to college students.
2. singing quietly	We noticed a small <u>child</u> in the corner.
3. leaping from rock to rock	It was difficult to catch up to the <u>woman</u>.
4. carrying only a knapsack on her back	My <u>friend</u> went to Europe.
5. taxing imports of foreign goods	Are you in favor of the <u>law</u>?
6. floating in the vial	The lab assistant carefully examined the <u>specimen</u>.

7. wondering if he would get the <u>Jeffrey</u> was unable to concentrate
   job   on his book.

_____

_____

Punctuation Review

a. Phrase following nonsubject: no comma usually needed.
b. Phrase coming before subject: set off by comma.
c. Identifying phrase after subject: no commas.
d. Nonidentifying phrase after subject: set off by commas.
e. Phrase referring to subject and
   coming at end of sentence: usually set off by comma.

B. Underline the participial phrase(s) in each sentence and add commas where necessary.

1. Franz taking a leave of absence from school traveled across the country for a year.

2. Peering through the fog we could see her across the road waving her hands at us.

3. The young man sighing deeply thought of his family so far away.

4. A lesson explaining the uses of the dictionary should be part of every reading course.

5. Substituting for the receptionist Juanita learned many things about the firm in just one week.

6. The waiter looked for the tip lying under the plate.

7. The baby crying in a middle row disturbed everyone in the movie theater.

8. A person living alone is no longer denied the right to adopt a child in some countries.

9. The lawyer was afraid of the judge trying the case.

10. Stumbling into the room I stopped when I saw everyone looking at me.

C. Rewrite the following sentences, changing the relative clauses (beginning with *who, which, or that*) to *-ing* participial phrases. Remember the rules for commas.

EXAMPLE
Thirty years ago airplanes that flew overhead were always noticed by everyone.

Thirty years ago airplanes flying overhead were always noticed by everyone.

1. Any musician who wins a prize in the Tchaikowsky competition can look forward to a good career.

_____

_____

2. Ms. Mitchell, who expected her friend for a visit, was surprised to see a stranger at the door.

_____

_____

3. The audience could hear the loud music that competed with the speaker.

_____

_____

4. This book, which deals with the causes of war, should be read by all who want to preserve peace.

_____

_____

5. The actor who performed Faust so well last night was unknown to me.

_____

_____

SCRAMBLED SENTENCES

The phrases in each sentence are not arranged in the right word order. Rearrange each group of words to form a meaningful sentence. This exercise will give you some practice with prepositional phrases. Always look first for nouns and verbs to go with them. Prepositions must have an object: a noun (in the *house*), a pronoun (for *me*), or a gerund (in *learning*).

1. on, the water, felt cold, my skin.

_____

_____

2. the house, where I lived, from, my way, I could find.

_____

_____

3. at, the tomato, splashed, my neck, the nape, of

_____

_____

4. at, stared, a man going, in, me, the opposite direction.

_____

_____

5. his shoulder, glancing back, and, over, he kept walking.

_____

_____

6. between, the difference, a block and, I already knew, a street.

_____

_____

7. across, the smoke, stopped, a chemical plant, the street, of, my breathing.

_____

_____

8. I had expected, with, money, a bag, to come along, of, someone.

_____

_____

9. the number, on, the end, toward, a man checked, each day, the meter, of.

_____

_____

10. was plaited, two braids, that stuck out, in, above, her hair, her ears.

_____

_____

SENTENCE COMBINING

Combine each pair of sentences into a single sentence using a participial phrase as a modifier.

EXAMPLE

a. He felt grateful to the United States.

b. He began to lecture on the advantages of American life.

Feeling grateful to the United States, he began to lecture on the advantages of American life.

1a. I was on my guard.

b. I was glancing back over my shoulder.

_____

_____

2a. The deep, prolonged siren of a steamboat was like a hand.

b. The hand was pulling at my heartstrings.

_____

_____

3a. I put my foot on the machine's treadle.

b. I started to feed the punch.

_____

_____

4a. The punch was piercing holes in the pieces of metal and bending them so that they looked like ears.

b. The punch went up and down.

_____

_____

5a. The sap was running from the eye of the slashed vine like tears from a human eye.

b. One could see the sap.

_____

_____

6a. I was crossing over into the block.
 b. I was struck with the tomato.

_____

_____

7a. She pushed back her black hair.
 b. She grinned at the foreigner.

_____

_____

8a. The tomato splashed on his neck.
 b. He felt the tomato on his neck.

_____

_____

9a. I learned the difference between a block and a street.
 b. I had been asking questions.

_____

_____

10a. The picture showed a real American.
 b. The American was drinking beer from a keg.

_____

_____

Writing Assignments

ESSAY TOPICS

Use at least three words from the vocabulary exercises.

1. Write a narrative description of your early experiences in the United States during your first day, your first week, or even your first month. What feeling did you have as you went from the airport to your new home? What caught your attention? Were you excited, surprised, pleased, or disappointed? What did you do as soon as you arrived? What experiences did you have in the following days?

2. Compare your present neighborhood with the one where you lived in your native country. You may wish to compare not only the immediate neighborhoods but also the larger cities or towns in which they are located. (To compare means to discuss both similarities and differences.)

3. Modern life is dehumanizing. Write an essay in which you agree or disagree with this statement.

4. Write an analysis of the reading passage, determining whether Christowe's first impressions of America were mainly positive or negative. You will find it easier to organize your ideas if you start your analysis by completing the following chart:

Positive	Negative
a. Earning good money.	a. Dehumanization of work.
b. Friendliness of the little black girl.	b. Having a tomato thrown at him.
c.	c.
d.	d.

You then can decide on the best method of writing about these points. You might discuss all the positive impressions first, then the negative ones, and then draw a conclusion. Another method is to discuss a positive point together with a corresponding negative point, then draw conclusions. Of course, you might not always find corresponding negative and positive points, which fact in itself would help you to come to a conclusion.

PROOFREADING

There are 13 errors in the following passage. Find and correct them. Note: Run-ons (comma splices) each count as one error.

My first week in America was one of the most interesting week I have ever lived through. I was assign to a nearby high school where I found that I wasn't only non-English-speaking student. Unfortunatly, none of my new classmates spoke my native language, however, I began make progress in English immediately. After school every days, a friend took me sightseeing. The shopping centers were very impressive, and the number of movies and theaters was overwhelming. There was also a few things that dissapointed me. One of them were the subway, which seemed to be the worse in the world. Other very disturbing thing was the poor condition of many neighborhoods. I didn't expected to see so many of them in such bad shape.

CHAPTER 3

Learning English

When I first arrived, I was really upset, because I had studied English in my own country, and yet I could not understand anything said to me.   I was glad that there were no French-speaking students in my class so that I had to speak English all the time.   In six months here, I learned more English than I had in three years at home.

From a Haitian student's paper.

READING PASSAGE

About the Author: After his first year in the United States, Salom Rizk left his job in a slaughterhouse to peddle oriental rugs from door to door in order to meet Americans and learn English.   Then he attended school, while working as a dishwasher, and eventually owned a successful shoe repair business.   He was so grateful for the opportunities he found in this country that during the depression he did free shoe repairing for the poor.   He began to speak to school and community groups about his experiences in Syria and about the virtues of America compared with the hardships of Europe.   Later he lectured for many years in every state in the nation under the sponsorship of *Reader's Digest.*

To Think About: As you read, try to answer the following questions.   (See page xiii for reading guidelines.)

1. What is the first problem in English pronunciation that Rizk discusses? (Your answer will be a main idea.)

2. According to Rizk, what was the real explanation for the difficulty of the English language? (Your answer will be a main idea.)

3. Rizk thought that the plural of *booth* was *beeth.*   Why? (Your answer will be a detail supporting a main idea.)

4. What were some advantages that young American schoolchildren took for granted? (Your answer will be a main idea.)

5. Why was Rizk's speech so successful? (Your answer will be an implication.)

From
SYRIAN YANKEE

SALOM RIZK

(After his first job in a meat-packing house, Salom Rizk peddled rugs and tapestries from door to door in Minnesota and Iowa, hoping that a summer's work would improve his English so that he could start school.)

My English was, if anything, more atrocious than ever. It was a polyglot* mixture of packing-house profanity, Syrianized slang, and sales chatter. In a desperate effort to shed* the profanity I took to substituting the word "Hello." It was an omnibus* expression providing emotional outlet for every type of explosion or distress. If something puzzled me, it was "Hello?" If something went terribly wrong, it was an angry, shouted "Hello!! Hello!!!" The most descriptive, overworked adjective in my vocabulary was "lousy." It was the universal word to describe all the extremes of good, bad, or indifferent size, height, weight, shape, color, quality, and quantity. Before the summer was over, everything was "lousy," including the English language—the way I spoke it.

(Salom decides that the only way to learn English properly is in school.)

It was decided to start me out in the fourth grade. Imagine how I felt, a grown man in long pants going to school with a bunch of kids. When the full force of this discrepancy* struck me, I knew I was not going to like school. I expected the youngsters to make fun of me, to laugh at my ignorance, my backwardness, and my awful accent. Strangely, nothing of the kind happened. Sometimes they would laugh at the way I scrambled the language, but it was not in ridicule.* It was all in good hearty fun which I enjoyed as much as they did.

Both my teachers and my little classmates were exceedingly helpful. My eagerness to learn the English language was equaled by the enthusiasm* of my teachers to help me. I was like a child learning his first words,

---

polyglot Context clues: the prefix *poly-*, meaning many; "mixture."

shed Context clue: "substituting."

omnibus Context clues: the prefix *omni-*, meaning all; "every type."

discrepancy Context clue: the implication of an enormous difference between a grown man and little kids.

ridicule Context clue: "to make fun of."

enthusiasm Context clue: "eagerness . . . equaled by."

and they almost applauded me every time I acquired a new word or turned a new sentence. My progress seemed to give them endless* pleasure, and this spurred me on to extra effort.

By applying myself in my spare time and through special tutoring from my teachers, I was able to move ahead rapidly. Every few weeks came a promotion* until, by the end of the semester, I was ready for ninth-grade English.

I hadn't worked long on the English language, however, before I was convinced I could not depend on logic to learn it. I thought at first it would be something like my native tongue, that if you learned the letters of the alphabet and their sounds, plus some rules of grammar and spelling, you could learn by yourself.

But I had not counted on the English language being so unreasonable. There was, for example, a whole mess of sounds which were not represented in the alphabet. So it seemed somebody had gone to the trouble to juggle* the letters until they fell into the most astonishing combinations, *ch, sh, ph, gh* being only among the least unpronounceable cases. After struggling for hours with certain alphabetical monstrosities, I was convinced that no one without English ancestors could ever hope to discover their sounds. But even worse than all this, when there was a very obvious letter in the alphabet to stand for a sound, somebody had labored to invent combinations which defied all my attempts at pronunciation. It was my habit to hunt in the dictionary for new words to add to my vocabulary, and one day I came across a real freak: "phthisic." How do you pronounce that? *Phth?* I find there is a simple letter in the alphabet to stand for the sound this four-letter behemoth is supposed to make. It is the letter *t*, twenty letters down in the alphabet and not so hard to find, either. Yet here is this *phth*, a monument to Anglo-Saxon* ingenuity—one sound, four letters, and you have to guess which one to pronounce. I used to puzzle no end* over words like "freight" and "weight," and I don't understand yet why the word "colonel" is mispronounced so badly. Many times I would despair of either learning or reforming a language which behaved so unreasonably.

And then I had to memorize a whole chaos of vowel sounds, long *a,* short *a,* broad *a,* etc., etc., etc. The letter *a,* in fact, was the worst offender, the black sheep* in the vowel family.* And a close second was his fat brother, the letter *o,* with six different noises to his credit. The letter *e,* with a little less criminal talent, has only five, yet it could be at times as wicked

---

endless   Context clue: the suffix *-less*, meaning without.

promotion   Context clue: "move ahead."

juggle   Context clue: "they fell into the most astonishing combinations."

Anglo-Saxon   Rizk thought that Anglo-Saxon was the only origin of the English language, but a word like *phthisic* also has French, Latin, and Greek origins.

no end   Endlessly, for a very long time.

black sheep   A person considered to be the most disgraceful member of a family.

vowel family   Rizk refers to vowels as if they were human members of a family, such as a brother or cousin.

as the worst. But the letter *i*—I have a special affection for the letter *i*. Of any letter in the English alphabet, it comes the nearest to being a second cousin of the Syrian vowels. It has only two sounds and does not require you to take singing lessons before you can hit them.

Pronouns used to give me a lot of trouble, too. I would puzzle over them a whole evening. They behaved with no more respect for law and order than the vowels or those distressing consonant combinations. It seemed to me that if it is right to say "he," "his," "him," why shouldn't it follow: "she," "shis," "shim"? But no. The pundits had to make it "she," "her," and "hers" and complicate the whole business of the immigrant trying to become a good American.

All these peculiarities made it infinitely harder for me to learn the language, and sometimes I was indignant with the anonymous fathers of a tongue which I could not learn by myself. I had to wait for my teacher or some friend to help me pronounce almost every single word.

I asked one of my teachers about all this.

"Are there no rules to the English language?"

"Yes, most certainly, there are rules," she assured me, "but there are exceptions to the rules."

But that did not seem to explain the difficulty. Later the real explanation came out: there were not only exceptions to the rules, but exceptions to the exceptions.

I was particularly bothered by the exceptions to the forming of plurals. I was told that the plural of any word was made by adding *s* or *es,* but when I made "foot" into "foots," I learned that was wrong. It was "feet," just as the plural of "tooth" is "teeth." Well, I had discovered a new rule. But when I made the word "booth" into "beeth," my teachers said the old rule applied, and it was "booths." By this time my mind was so full of confusion that I was almost in a mood to stick to my native Syrian.

I went on to learn to my astonishment that "mouse" does not become "mouses" the way "house" becomes "houses" and that it is never right to say "hice" for the plural of "house" the way you say "mice" for the plural of "mouse" or "lice" for the plural of "louse." But how was I supposed to tell? The plural of "sheep" is neither "sheeps" nor "shoop," but "sheep," just like the singular, right straight through to ten million or even a billion billion of them. But a "baby beef" in the herd* is not "baby beef" or "baby beefs" or "baby boofs," but "baby beeves." They told me that "ox" does not become "oxes" as "box" becomes "boxes." Then, when I thought I had found a clue, namely, that live things form different plurals from inanimate* things, and proceeded to make "foxen" out of "fox," the teachers told me I was wrong again. They said it was "foxes." What was I to do? I was ready to appeal to the legislature for a law and make it just plain "oxen" and "foxen" and "boxen."

---

herd Context clues: "ten million"; the idea of plurals.

inanimate Context clues: opposite of "live"; the prefix *in-,* meaning not.

At last there was nothing for me to do but to memorize all this and get used to it. But sometimes I revolted, especially when my ignorance of how to spell or pronounce the language brought me embarrassment.

One day I was ordering a meal in a restaurant. It was just before the repeal of prohibition.* On the menu they had "spiced tomato juice." I had just learned that the letter *c* is sometimes pronounced hard, as in "cat." So after studying for a while I ordered "spiked* tomato juice" and was icily informed that they did not serve liquor there.

During this first year in school came one of my greatest astonishments: that Americans—especially young schoolgoing Americans—took their many blessings and opportunities so much for granted. That everybody could speak and write and worship as he pleased did not seem strange to anybody. That education was free for everyone down to the humblest of citizens amazed no one. In Ain Arab I used to long for just one sheet of paper to write on. I hungered for just one book to read, one book to call my own, and I used to rescue scraps of Syrian newspaper from the gutters of Beirut, take them home, and feast on them a whole evening. But here in America books and papers were everywhere, the schools were as magnificent* as palaces, and the equipment comfortable, stimulating, breathtaking. I was fascinated by all the richness, the maps and pictures on the walls, the great blackboards, all the high windows, and the many lights which were turned on when it was cloudy outdoors. How could anyone take all this grand achievement for granted?

I saw these precious privileges and opportunities wasted by too many young Americans who evidently could not comprehend what my experience had forced upon me: the difference, the unbelievable contrast,* between that old world their forefathers had left and this new world they had built. I saw youngsters actually despising the school and what it stood for, showing contempt for those who were brighter or studied harder than they did. I saw them playing hooky,* pretending sickness, "getting by" with as little learning as possible. Some of them boasted of their skill in cheating and laughed up their sleeves* at their unwitting teachers. They disfigured the beautiful surroundings lavished upon them, carving their initials on the furniture and marking up the walls.

I could not understand at first how anyone could be so heedless, so negligent, and even contemptuous of these hard-won common possessions. I learned how the ancestors of these students had worked and fought and sacrificed for the rights they took so much for granted. The more I dug into American history, reading much of it in the Syrian language, the greater became my astonishment. I felt that I ought to do something to

---

prohibition Refers to the Eighteenth Amendment to the U.S. Constitution (1920–1933), which prohibited the sale of alcoholic beverages.

spiked Context clue: "liquor."

magnificent Context clue: "palaces."

contrast Context clue: "difference."

playing hooky Context clue: "pretending sickness."

laughed up their sleeves Laughed secretly.

awaken my fellow Americans to all these blessings. I now had a powerful new incentive* to learn the language of the country of which I was fortunate enough to be a citizen.

Strangely, I did not recognize my first opportunity to discuss appreciation of American democracy, and only gradually did it dawn upon me that I had found the avenue which was to become a career for me. It happened this way. One day the teacher asked the class to write a theme.

"But I cannot write," I told her.

"You can talk, though, can't you, Sam?" she said, smiling at me.

"Yes, I can talk a little, but I can't write themes."

"Suppose that, instead of writing a theme, you tell us your story."

"Tell my story?"

"Yes, tell us something about yourself, your life in Syria, how you found out you were an American, your struggles to reach this country, and how you feel about things. You don't have to make it long, and I know it will be interesting to all of us."

The more I thought of that assignment, the more it terrified me. I had never stood before an audience in my life. I had told my teacher that my talk would be lousy, and I was sure it would. I looked forward to the ordeal* with the same misgivings which torment a soldier the first time he goes into the firing line.

Four days later I stood before nearly forty youngsters. My knees promptly became as weak as jelly, my tongue as heavy as a mountain, my

---

incentive Context clue: the meaning of the previous sentence.

ordeal Context clues: "terrified"; "torment a soldier."

throat dry. My hands felt as big as those packing-house hams. After an eternity of silence, during which I adjusted my hands and feet in all the awkward positions I could think of, my tongue came free and I began to use it. The first thing I said was, "Hello!" Everybody laughed.

Twenty-five minutes later I sat down, hardly aware of the time that had passed. The youngsters were clamoring for more. But the ordeal was over. I had not imagined that anyone could forget himself so completely. Speaking and sleeping have at least one thing in common: when you get through you don't know just how long you've been at them.

Within the next few weeks I addressed nearly all the classes in the school. My teacher told the other teachers, and they invited me to repeat my story to their pupils. With each telling my confidence mounted. Each time I tried to use a wider range of words, tried to get the feel of phrases which would mean the most to the youngsters. All these opportunities to speak were a great encouragement to me and gave my tussles with the English language extra motive and determination. When the teachers began to tell me how they were awakened to a new appreciation of their American blessings, I began to see my story as the answer to the desire growing within me.

Comprehension

These questions are to be answered orally or in writing. Some of them may require more than one sentence for your answer.

1. What were two situations in which Rizk incorrectly used the word "Hello"?
2. What surprised Rizk when he started school in the fourth grade?
3. How long did it take Rizk to go from the fourth grade to the ninth?
4. According to Rizk, why would it be possible to learn Syrian by oneself?
5. What is the first problem in English pronunciation that Rizk discusses?
6. What was difficult about the pronunciation of English vowels?
7. Why did Rizk have a special affection for the letter *i*?
8. Why did pronouns trouble Rizk?
9. According to Rizk, what was the real explanation for the difficulty of the English language?
10. Rizk thought that the plural of "booth" was "beeth." Why?
11. What was Rizk's reason for believing that the plural of "fox" was "foxen"?
12. What was Rizk's final solution to the problem of spelling and pronunciation?
13. What were some advantages that young American schoolchildren took for granted?
14. In what ways did some young Americans show that they did not appreciate their opportunities?
15. What was Rizk's new incentive to learn English?
16. What did Rizk's teacher suggest he do instead of writing a theme?
17. What did Rizk find out about the ordeal of making a speech?
18. Why was Rizk's speech so successful?

DISCUSSION QUESTIONS

1. When you were first learning English, were there a few words that you used all the time? What meanings did you have for those words? In what situations did you use them? Are there any such words that you still continue to use frequently?
2. What has given you the most difficulty in learning English? Discuss in detail what you find hard, such as the formation of plurals, verb forms, and spelling. For example, if it is pronunciation, discuss which sounds are most difficult for you and why.
3. How is the English used in advertisements, signs, and newspaper head-

lines different from the language used in books, magazines, and the main parts of newspapers? Have these differences caused you any trouble or difficulty?

4. Some colleges give full credit for learning English as a second language; others give only part or no credit at all. Which system do you believe is correct and why?

5. What is the relationship between speaking, writing, and reading a second language? Do you have to be able to speak a language in order to read it or write it? Is reading necessary for speaking or writing? Does writing help speaking or reading? Which have you found the most difficult? Should they be learned in a particular order or all at once?

CLOZE EXERCISE

Fill in each blank with a single (one) word.

By applying myself _____ my spare time _____ through special tutoring _____ my teachers, I _____ able to move _____ rapidly. Every few _____ came a promotion _____, by the end _____ the semester, I _____ ready for ninth grade _____.

I hadn't worked _____ on the English _____, however, before I _____ convinced I could _____ depend on logic _____ learn it. I _____ at first it _____ be something like _____ native tongue, that _____ you learned the _____ of the alphabet _____ their sounds, plus _____ rules of grammar _____ spelling, you could _____ by yourself.

VOCABULARY

WORD FORMS

Fill in the blanks with the correct forms of the word given for each group sentences. You may need the verb (changed where necessary for agreement or tense), participles, a noun (singular or plural), an adjective, or an adverb. For example:

project

a. One of his teeth <u>projects</u> beyond his lip. (*verb form*)

b. The building <u>project</u> was abandoned for lack of funds. (*noun*)

c. The school could not purchase a film <u>projector</u> because it was too expensive. (*noun form*)

1. profane

a. In that school, the children are not allowed to use _____ language.

b. _____ in the movies is no longer censored as it once was.

c. She speaks _____ of her former husband.

2. weigh

a. Someone stole my suitcases just before they _____ at the airline counter.

b. It is difficult to discuss important, _____ matters in an atmosphere of confusion.

c. Marina put on some _____ during her vacation.

d. He _____ too much in proportion to his height.

3. ignore

a. He used to _____ me when were both going to college.

b. We should not have to suffer because of the _____ of our leaders.

c. Some people are _____ of what is happening in the world today.

4. enthusiastic

a. He was able to pass the course because of the _____ of his teachers in helping him.

b. My older brother is extremely _____ about sports.

c. She was working _____ on her project when I came in.

5. promote

a. The UN is an organization that _____ world peace.

b. His father was given a _____ from policeman to detective.

c. Mr. Charles is the sales _____ of a book company.

6. represent

a. We elected a _____ from our house to the block association.

b. She _____ both men and women equally in the Congress.

c. The student demonstrators demanded _____ in the Faculty Senate.

7. **astonish**

a. Mr. Garcia has the most _____ collection of miniature dolls.

b. The audience was _____ by the skill of the gymnasts.

c. Mary and John had been going steady for a long time, but to my

_____ she married Robert.

8. **reform**

a. Some political movements believe in _____ rather than in complete change of the system.

b. The administrators consider _____ the school very difficult.

c. He is a _____ alcoholic.

d. Martin Luther was responsible for the _____ which produced the Protestant religions.

9. **confuse**

a. The child was _____ by the crowds at the circus.

b. College registration can be very _____ for freshmen.

c. The case was not solved because of _____ among the witnesses.

d. A beginning dancer often _____ the right foot with the left.

10. **embarrass**

a. He asked her an _____ question that made her blush.

b. Some teachers _____ their students in front of the whole class.

c. Beverly caused _____ by making a scene at the party last night.

d. I was _____ by the concern everyone showed for me.

11. **prohibit**

a. Is it possible to _____ the use of alcohol and drugs by the young?

b. For many years, the _____ amendment made the sale of liquor illegal.

c. Her parents _____ her from going out alone late at night until she was twenty-one.

12. **magnificent**

a. Versailles is one of the most _____ palaces in Europe.

b. He behaved _____ all through his severe illness.

c. The _____ of the Great Wall of China is indescribable.

13. **stimulate**

   a. His lectures are always very _____.

   b. Reading both _____ and relaxes the mind.

   c. An opera by Puccini was responsible for the _____ of his interest in music.

14. **encourage**

   a. The senator was very _____ by the response to his speech.

   b. Because of the _____ of her teachers, she decided to study law.

   c. Your excellent cooking unfortunately _____ me to overeat.

   d. The first flower is always an _____ sign of spring.

15. **appreciate**

   a. Linda developed an _____ of art while in high school.

   b. Your immediate reply to this letter will be very much _____.

   c. My friend was very _____ when I helped him find a job in the school.

   d. Many people _____ not _____ the pleasures of the country.

SYNONYMS

Rewrite each sentence choosing an appropriate synonym from the list below for each underlined word or phrase.

1. convince	6. defy	11. rescue
2. ingenuity	7. appeal	12. discrepancy
3. contempt	8. anonymous	13. attempts
4. chaos	9. obvious	14. inanimate
5. distress	10. exceedingly	15. motive

1. The girl was in great <u>sorrow and suffering</u> when her mother died.

_____

_____

2. Their five-year-old daughter swims <u>extremely</u> well.

_____

_____

3. I was not able to <u>persuade</u> him to go with me to the Far East.

_____

_____

4. It was very <u>clear and plain</u> which team would lose the game.

_____

_____

5. A hostess <u>tries</u> to make everybody feel comfortable in her house.

_____

_____

6. My English teacher gave us a poem written by an <u>unknown</u> author.

_____

_____

7. The lifeguard came immediately to <u>save</u> the boy from the attack of the shark.

_____

_____

8. The success of the program is based on her <u>skill and cleverness</u> in dealing with people.

_____

_____

9. The new bookkeeper had to straighten out the <u>total confusion</u> in the firm's records.

_____

_____

10. He deserves <u>scorn</u> for his treatment of his parents.

_____

_____

11. The <u>underlying reason</u> for his unfriendliness was fear of being hurt.

_____

_____

12. There was an <u>inconsistency</u> between the stories of the two witnesses.

_____

_____

13. Prepositions seem to <u>resist</u> all my attempts to understand them.

_____

_____

14. Some <u>lifeless</u> objects, like paintings, seem to be alive.

_____

_____

15. I made an <u>urgent request</u> to my employer for a raise in salary.

_____

_____

Grammar

PRESENT PARTICIPIAL PHRASES II

Misplaced and Dangling Participial Phrases

As we saw in Present Participial Phrases I (page 36), participial phrases contain a verb with the -*ing* ending and modify or refer to nouns or pronouns. It is important that the -*ing* phrase be placed close enough to the word it refers to, so that no misunderstanding or awkwardness occurs.

EXAMPLE
We tried to attract the attention of the policeman, <u>shouting loudly</u>.

To avoid the possibility that it is the policeman who is shouting, the sentence should read:

<u>Shouting loudly</u>, we tried to attract the attention of the policeman.

Sometimes the participial phrase is not merely misplaced, but actually has no place because there is no word in the sentence for it to modify. Note such a "dangling" phrase in the following:

The trees were beautiful <u>walking along the country road</u>.

Since the trees obviously could not have been walking, the sentence must be reworded. A possible alternative is:

<u>Walking along the country road</u>, I thought the trees were beautiful.

GRAMMAR EXERCISES

A. Rewrite the following sentences to correct the misplaced or dangling participial phrases.

1. Rumbling and squeaking, I worked so hard I was not aware of the machine.

_____

_____

2. Not knowing the language, the instructions were impossible to read.

_____

_____

3. Giving a dull speech, the audience started to walk out on the chairman.

_____

_____

4. Painting the walls, the room looked much better.

_____

_____

5. Staring at words in the newspaper, they had no meaning to me.

_____

_____

6. Suppressing her tears, the crowd watched the woman.

_____

_____

7. Believing in freedom of speech, his ideas made sense.

_____

_____

8. Walking into the room, everybody there turned to look at me.

_____

_____

9. Dying from hunger, the food tasted wonderful to the man.

_____

_____

10. Holding the whip in her hand, the wild dog did not attack the young woman.

_____

_____

B. Time Words. Some participial phrases may begin with a time word, such as *after, before, while,* or *when.*

EXAMPLE

<u>After</u> struggling for hours with certain words, I was convinced that no one could understand their pronunciation.

Change the time clauses in the following sentences to participial phrases, keeping the time word.

EXAMPLE

Before he worked as a rug peddler, Rizk killed animals in a slaughterhouse.
<u>Before working as a rug peddler,</u> Rizk killed animals in a slaughterhouse.

1. After I had studied the menu for a while, I ordered "spiked tomato juice."

_____

_____

2. While he was attending school, Rizk earned his living as a dishwasher.

_____

_____

3. When he wrote his autobiography, he had to relive many painful memories.

_____

_____

4. While he was still losing money in his business, he repaired shoes free for the poor.

_____

_____

5. Before he worked for _Reader's Digest,_ Rizk obtained many speaking engagements through his own efforts.

_____

_____

C. Participial phrases are of value in providing variety in sentence structure and reducing wordiness. Rewrite the following sentences using a participial phrase.

EXAMPLE

Unemployment has increased steadily and is approaching a rate of 9 percent.

Increasing steadily, unemployment is approaching a rate of 9 percent.

1. In some colleges, students earn credit for work experience while they continue to take courses.

_____

_____

2. Many readers are trying to help their libraries and are contributing money for expenses.

_____

_____

3. Since he knew very little English, he was unable to find a good job.

_____

_____

4. As the astronaut prepares for his launching, he makes sure that all his equipment is in order.

_____

_____

5. Since the professor gives her students help and encouragement, she expects them to do all the work required.

_____

_____

6. Some New Yorkers, who pay very high taxes, want commuters to be taxed also.

_____

_____

7. Because of various space projects, there are now many satellites and other objects that orbit around the earth.

_____

_____

8. Many different flus, which originated in specific countries, have now spread all over the world.

_____

_____

9. Because Sagittarians take an interest in people, they often become doctors or psychologists.

_____

_____

10. Americans consume large quantities of soft drinks that contain caffeine.

_____

_____

SCRAMBLED SENTENCES

The phrases in each sentence are not arranged in the right word order. Rearrange each group of words to form a meaningful sentence. This exercise will give you practice in the order of adjectives before a noun.

1. neat, city of Iowa, we landed, little, in a

_____

_____

2. around the campus, cool, we drove, roads, winding, over the

_____

_____

3. overworked, was "lousy," word, the most, in my vocabulary, descriptive

_____

_____

4. shouted, I used a(n), "Hello," angry, when upset

_____

_____

5. to learn English, the writer, new, had a, incentive, powerful

_____

_____

6. electrical, equipment, comfortable, the schools here, modern, have

_____

_____

7. accompanied him, huge, on the fifth floor, room, the elevator man, freezing, to a

_____

_____

8. Syrian-looking, muscular, fellow, he was teamed with, young, who chewed tobacco, a

_____

_____

9. speech, fine, delivered, long, the boy, forceful, a

_____

_____

SENTENCE COMBINING

Use *who, which, why,* or *that* to combine two sentences into one. If you wish to use other connectors, feel free to do so. You may find more than one possibility in some cases.

1a. I had told my teacher.
  b. My talk would not be good.

_____

_____

2a. I don't understand yet.
  b. The word "colonel" is mispronounced so badly.

_____

_____

3a. Somebody had labored to invent combinations of letters.
  b. These combinations defied all my attempts at pronunciation.

_____

_____

4a. I would despair of learning a language.
  b. The language behaved so unreasonably.

_____

_____

5a. Sometimes I was indignant with the language.
  b. I could not learn the language by myself.

_____

_____

6a. I was informed.
  b. They did not serve liquor here.

_____

_____

7a. I had found a schoolmaster.
  b. He would help me to learn the language of America.

_____

_____

8a. I was fascinated by all the high windows and the many lights.
  b. These lights were turned on when it was cloudy outdoors.

_____

_____

9a. I tried to get the feel of phrases.
  b. These phrases would mean the most to the audience.

_____

_____

10a. I had found the opportunity.
  b. The opportunity was to become a career for me.

_____

_____

Writing Assignments

ESSAY TOPICS

Use at least three words from the vocabulary exercises.

1. Discuss how you have learned English. What did you learn from school, what from talking to people, what from signs on the street, newspapers, records, television, and advertisements?
2. Compare your own language with English. Discuss some similarities and differences. Which language do you think is more logical and why? Choose one or two aspects to compare, such as pronunciation, the writing system, pronouns, plurals, or any other points in grammar.
3. Describe an incident that took place in a restaurant, department store, or some other public place, when someone misunderstood what you said

or you misunderstood another person. How did you resolve the difficulty?

4. Write an argument in which you support a position on the question of granting credit for college courses in English as a Second Language. Do you think full, part, or no credit should be given?

Suggested Outline

A. Introduction
   1. You might explain the background necessary to understand the problem. For example, why has it become an issue in recent years?
   2. You might show what areas of agreement already exist on the subject. For example, most colleges do accept the necessity of having courses in ESL.
B. Give examples to support your position and draw a conclusion from them. For example, you may be able to obtain some information on how many colleges give credit and how much.
C. Present a comparison pattern of argument in which you give the advantages of your proposal and the disadvantages of the opposite view.
D. Take into account possible objections to your proposal and give reasons why these objections are wrong or unimportant. (This is called a *refutation.*)
E. Conclusion: Sum up your main arguments and the benefits to be achieved from your proposal.

PROOFREADING

There are 13 errors in the following passage. Find and correct them. Note: Misused infinitives each count as one error.

The ability to aquire English depend to a great extent on the background of the family. When I was eleven years old, I was very eager to learn English. I was help by my father, who taught me how to pronounce and spell words. As the years go on, I could read a lot and increased my vocabulary. When I finished the high school, I insisted to enter a college that used English as the main language. There, I learn how to use proper English in reading and writting. Above all, I learned thousand of medical terms.

When I came to this country, I could understand everyone very well. I tried and still trying very hard to improve my English. At the beginning, I could not read the newspaper because it had a lot of abbrevations and difficult words, but after few months, I learned by myself how to read the newspaper, and now I enjoy to read any article.

CHAPTER 4

On the Job

My first day on the job was a disaster.   As a beginner, I expected some consideration from the boss, but he wanted me to get acquainted with the work in one day.   The other employees weren't friendly at all. When I asked them something, they would hardly open their mouths to help me.

From a Spanish student's paper.

READING PASSAGE

About the Author: After a good education in his native Korea (which is described in an earlier book, *The Grass Roof*), Younghill Kang continued his studies in the United States.   He supported himself by taking so many different jobs that it is not surprising to learn how varied his later career was—as teacher, writer, museum consultant, lecturer, and adviser to the American Military Government in Korea.

To Think About: As you read, try to answer the following questions. (See page xiii for reading guidelines.)

1. In describing his job experiences, the author usually comes to some conclusion about each one.   What are these different conclusions? (Your answers will be the author's opinions and conclusions.)

2. Younghill Kang is Korean.   However, is Korean the only language he understands?   How do you know?
   (Your answer will be supporting details.)

3. What is one major idea or theme that seems to run through Younghill's description of his jobs?   (This is *not* the same question as 1.)
   (Your answer will be an implication about the main idea of the passage.)

From
EAST GOES WEST

YOUNGHILL KANG

(Younghill Kang first gets a job as a servant in a wealthy woman's house where he is treated "like a dog or cat" and is soon fired because he sleeps too late one morning. Next, he works as a clerk in a store owned by Sung, a Chinese importer.)

Soon Sung complained that I was taking too long for my lunch, that I was coming too late in the morning, more especially, that I was not using enough imagination in naming the price to a customer. He said, "In charging, use your own judgment. The ticket is merely to go by.* Study psychology. If they are willing to pay, charge high. If not, sell some way."

This was the reason he never marked the right price in English, although it was a store only for Americans and no Oriental customers ever came there. He always used Chinese scripts scribbled on the bottom of the goods to indicate their approximate* value.

The big quarrel began when he saw me selling a shawl to a lady who had a limousine with a chauffeur. This shawl had been displayed in the window for a long time. The lady had noticed it and, having made up her mind, came in to buy it at once. She did not even ask the price until I was tying it up.

"How much?" she said then.

"$5.50," I said, which was marked on the tag in Chinese for me to tell by.

She paid that amount and went out.

Sung all the while was watching from the back of the store. He came up and his hair, so smooth usually, bristled like an angry cat's, while the little veins on his bald temples* twitched.

"That is not the way to do business," he said quietly, but with glinting eyes.

He was quiet for several minutes afterward, walking around the shop, touching this and that, though all was neat. He came back to me.

Adapted from *East Goes West* by Younghill Kang. Copyright © 1965 by Younghill Kang. Used by permission of Follett Publishing Company.

---

to go by To use as a guide.

approximate Context clue: the meaning of the previous paragraph. Is he being given an exact value?

temples Be sure you pick the right meaning from the dictionary, or this sentence will have a very strange meaning!

"If you don't learn American business methods, you will never do* here."

"What did I do wrong?" I said.

Then he told me I should have charged that rich lady much more for her shawl. I argued back. We had a fight. I left.

(Kang then finds work as a waiter.)

Fairly good American meals were served as well as chop-suey and chow mein; and since I did not like chow mein, I always took the American ones, with the addition of rice instead of bread and potatoes. The first day I worked hard to familiarize myself with the menu and all the different dishes the cook made. There seemed a lot of nuts—almond nuts, walnuts, leechee nuts, peanuts; a lot of sauce—Chinese sauce, Worcestershire sauce, tomato sauce, applesauce; a lot of creams—soup-cream, chicken-cream, vegetable-cream, ice-cream . . . so it impressed me strongly as a nut, sauce and cream restaurant. Not much else. But as a Chinese restaurant, it was thoroughly popularized. No electric sign for an eating place was more brilliant than the bright varicolored lights outside, encircling this up-stairs chop-suey place. There was a space for dancing in the middle of the floor, smooth and waxed. Once while running in to the kitchen, one of the waiters fell down with dishes and oil sauce on the floor, and even before he could wipe it up, one of the dancers fell down too, a fat man with a featherweight of a girl on top.

An American orchestra played constantly at that time, competing with the clatter of dishes and the roar of Broadway outside; then the place became like Grand Central Station with people hurrying from four quarters to catch trains. All sorts and conditions of people came to be fed on our hybrid* food.

Once in a while people who seemed impressive did not tip well. This matter of a tip, of course, was very absorbing. Who could avoid being glad at finding a fifty-cent piece or even a dollar on the table, like picking gold up from the street or fishing for it in the sea? At first you feel ashamed to take it. Then you take it with boredom as a matter of course.* Then you get caught up* to speculate to yourself. Then you talk to others about it, and by and by, the first thing you look for is the tip under the soiled plate. Sometimes it is large; sometimes it is small; occasionally nothing is there. You can never calculate—unless you are very clever, like some who had their rules by which a good tipper could be recognized, or one more than usually tight.* The tip has nothing to do with* the amount of service ren-

---

will never do   Will never be suitable; will never fit in.

hybrid   Is this word being used literally or as a metaphor? (See page 36.)

as a matter of course   An ordinary thing; nothing special.

get caught up   Get involved.

tight   Stingy.

has nothing to do with   Is not related to; does not depend on.

dered; it is all in the luck—like shooting craps, or playing the Chinese lottery. But it makes you size up* all people in terms of the tip they will bestow.

Waiting was really very hard work. And you had to have a gift for* it. During rush hours it was like a combination of skating and juggling. Some could carry four or five glasses in one hand and a heavy tray in the other . . . all while running crookedly through all the aisles made by the chairs. I did not have the gift for doing this, although I thought at the time it looked easy. I had been a good dancer at my uncle's birthday party. But now when I tried to carry only two things in one hand, water and a plate of soup, some of the soup slipped into a red-haired lady's lap. She talked very loud, almost crying. I said nothing.

"He doesn't understand English," said her brunette friend. "Get the boss."

Yes, I understood what she said, all right, but one does not say much when embarrassed. "I'm sorry" is not enough.

The boss came over. Both women repeated at once what I had done. Her green satin dress had a big spot. She pointed it out, over and over again. The boss looked at it through his spectacles. In the end, she was to charge the restaurant what it would cost to have this dress dry-cleaned. Peace was made, and she calmed her temper down.

But I was fired for that. It was not my first offense. I had broken a few dishes before too, and I had read Shakespeare and talked too much Chinese poetry. Without saying more the boss paid me off* and told me I need not come tomorrow. I did not dislike him for that. He was a good man. Business is business, not charity. I understood that I did not square with* American efficiency.

(*Kang's next job is in a hotel kitchen where he works as a helper, cutting grapefruits and handing out butter, sugar, salt, celery, and olives to the waiters.*)

I was on duty from four in the afternoon until around eleven at night. All the helpers were eating perpetually, just to relieve the monotony of the work. Everybody working here was fat. This was the kingdom of food, like the kingdom of the Drunk Land immortalized by Chinese poets. There was another helper, a boy about twenty, who was always chasing to and from the refrigerators a girl who worked in another department. At the refrigerators, he would get to hug the girl and could also snatch a bite of white chicken or cold meat. Even the kissing here, I thought, had to be done in the presence of lobster and mayonnaise! In my department, too, where there was not much chance for anything substantial, one did a fair amount of nibbling.* In cutting grapefruits a good deal of juice could be

---

to size up   To judge.

a gift for   A talent or an ability for.

paid off   Paid everything that was owed.

to square with   To fit into.

nibbling   Context clue: From the meaning of the sentence, it relates to eating but not "anything substantial."

caught in a cup and you always had the centers to suck. Cherries went on the grapefruits, and I ate a lot of cherries. As for melons, they provided much without giving cost to anybody, for what was left from fixing those generous portions had to be thrown out anyway.

Every once in a while at the hotel there would be a banquet. A banquet it was indeed, even for those lined up at the back door, the extra helpers. Sometimes as many as twenty additional hands* were called in. At a banquet—behind the scenes* at least—nobody seemed to get tired of eating, ever. I could see why the extra helpers ate. They all looked so thin and underfed. I think they had no other job. Day after day, they just waited for banquets. Maybe they called at all the big hotels. Maybe they hunted garbage, I don't know. Sometimes of course there would be two or even three banquets a week during the height of the season.* But then there would come long stretches of vacant days. Nothing doing. I know they made calls every day at the New Hotel where I served, to find if by any chance banquets were going on. Still, even when the great occasion came, the hotel had to turn many away. A great many more extras always applied than there was any need for.

We worked by the service door to receive the plates before passing them on to the dishwashing machines. Sometimes the dishes came out from the banquet with whole half-chickens and big pieces of steak or legs of duck intact. By rights* these must pass in a steady stream into the garbage can. Oh, how that garbage can was buttered! Butter on practically everything, even on fat steak or creamy vegetables. How rich and juicy and luxurious the French cook had made all these to feed the garbage can!

The rule was against stealing time, not food, and it was still possible to grab a piece of that chicken on the march to the garbage can if it could go in the mouth all at once. (No rule there about chewing while on the job!) Or sometimes, with lightning speed, half a chicken with only the breast taken off was slipped into a coat pocket.

Back-door banquets impressed me deeply, and I could never cease wondering. All the food passing along through hungry hands to feed the garbage pail . . . it was so wasteful, so fantastic, so American! . . . I always felt unusually depressed after a banquet. Not because I had to stay up until three or four in the morning. I was glad of that, because then I received extra pay. But there seemed some hitch* in American business methods. Why, you could feed more people with the waste food than those who had already been fed!

---

hands   Each "hand" means one worker (even though a person has two hands!).

behind the scenes   An expression taken from the theater and used to indicate a situation hidden by what is presented to public view.

height of the season   The busiest part of the season.

by rights   Properly.

hitch   Something that goes wrong.

(Kang's next job is entirely different. He works on a farm during the summer.)

Life was almost harshly simple.* And it was not easy. My work most of the time was hoeing, hoeing the corn, the potatoes and other crops in the garden. It must be done about eleven or twelve in the morning when the sun is high and hot, and it seemed to me the hardest work of all. That sun was merciless. Farmer Higgins and I and even Mrs. Higgins, we all had faces baked like cake with little cracks. Yes, farming, if you do it only a few hours a day, is a wholesome pleasure. But if you do it all the day long, getting up very early and not stopping until sundown, then it is very hard work. There are so many elements to watch, the sky, the insect-breeding land, the weeds, the fruit that must be picked when exactly ripe. Then the bird enemies must be constantly chased away. With his old clothes, Farmer Higgins made another Farmer Higgins* and stood him up in the fields as sentinel for the crows. Always one must be watching, and working, every minute.

Mr. Higgins kept saying with satisfaction that this year was going to be a good one. A full year meant a farmer could make a small nest egg for the shoes, hats, and winter clothes needed, perhaps store a little surplus in that local bank account, hoarding it up for the lean years.* But even so I saw that Farmer Higgins on his small farm could never make anything like prosperity or luxury. And though the Higginses were master and mistress, they worked harder than I who was the hired man. There were never any loafing days, not even Saturday or Sunday. Well, Sundays were free for me, but not for Farmer Higgins or Mrs. Higgins. There were the milking, the feeding of chickens, horses, pigs, and cows . . . all seeming to occur on a farm very often.

I thought of Farmer Higgins often in connection with the farmers of Asia. No doubt in Asia he might have been accounted a prosperous* man, and many others would be working for him. At least, he was never in danger of famine or starvation, and he by himself was able to produce more than a hundred Chinese farmers could produce. This was because of his labor-saving devices, though he did not even know that he was living in the Machine Age.

---

simple Note that one of the dictionary meanings for *simple* is "easy." However, here the author makes it clear that he is not using that meaning of *simple* but instead "plain, not luxurious."

another Farmer Higgins Context clues: "with his old clothes" and "sentinel for the crows."

lean years Context clue: contrasted with "full year" and "surplus."

prosperous Context clue: The meaning of the entire paragraph should give a clue to the meaning of the word.

Comprehension

These questions are to be answered orally or in writing. Some of them may require more than one sentence for your answer.

1. What were some of the complaints made by the store owner, Mr. Sung, against Younghill?
2. How did Mr. Sung decide on the actual selling price of his merchandise?
3. What did Younghill do wrong in selling the shawl to the lady?
4. What are some of the dishes the cook made in the restaurant? Are you familiar with them?
5. What made the restaurant popular?
6. Was the restaurant doing good business? How do you know?
7. In what way did Younghill change his mind about receiving tips?
8. Was Younghill usually able to know in advance how much tip he would receive? What did it depend on?
9. Why was the author fired from the restaurant?
10. How did he feel about being fired?
11. Aside from banquets, was the work in the hotel kitchen interesting? How do you know?
12. Judging from Younghill's description of the banquet, do you think there was a high or low employment rate at the time? Give reasons for your opinion.
13. What does "back-door banquets" mean?
14. Why did Younghill always feel unusually depressed after a banquet?
15. Did Younghill like farming? Why?
16. What must farmers always be watching? Why?
17. What do farmers usually do when they have a full year?
18. Even if Farmer Higgins had a lean year, why was he better off than the farmers of Asia?
19. What is one major idea or theme that seems to run through Younghill's descriptions of his jobs?

DISCUSSION QUESTIONS

1. Mr. Sung tells Younghill that he must learn American business methods. What methods does Mr. Sung mean? Are these methods particularly American, or are they found in other countries? What kind of business methods are practiced in your country?
2. Discuss the service you have received in restaurants. Do you get the

same kind of treatment if you go to a restaurant in your own country? Is there a relationship between the cost of the meal and the kind of service given?

3. What kind of tipper are you? Is the size of your tip related to the quality of the service rendered? Do you feel obliged to tip even if service is bad? Discuss the tipping customs in your country. (Do not limit the discussion to tipping in restaurants only.)

4. The author seemed to think that no skills were necessary for the job of waiter but then found out differently. Have you had this same experience where you discovered after you took a job that you did not have the necessary skills? Are there any jobs for which no skills are needed? If so, would you want these jobs?

5. What does Younghill's description of the banquets tell us about the distribution of wealth in the United States at that time (in the 1930s)? Has the situation changed since then? Is there an equal or unequal distribution of wealth in your own country?

CLOZE EXERCISE

Fill in each blank with a single (one) word.

Every once in a ＿＿＿＿＿ at the hotel there ＿＿＿＿＿ be a banquet. A ＿＿＿＿＿ it was indeed, even ＿＿＿＿＿ those lined up at ＿＿＿＿＿ back door, the extra ＿＿＿＿＿. Sometimes as many as ＿＿＿＿＿ additional hands were called ＿＿＿＿＿. At a banquet—behind ＿＿＿＿＿ scenes at least—nobody ＿＿＿＿＿ to get tired of ＿＿＿＿＿, ever. I could see ＿＿＿＿＿ the extra helpers ate. ＿＿＿＿＿ all looked so thin ＿＿＿＿＿ underfed. I think they ＿＿＿＿＿ no other job. Day ＿＿＿＿＿ day, they just waited ＿＿＿＿＿ banquets. Maybe they called ＿＿＿＿＿ all the big hotels. ＿＿＿＿＿ they hunted garbage, I ＿＿＿＿＿ know. Sometimes of course ＿＿＿＿＿ would be two or ＿＿＿＿＿ three banquets a week ＿＿＿＿＿ the height of the ＿＿＿＿＿.

Vocabulary

WORD FORMS

Fill in the blanks with the correct forms of the word given for each group of sentences. You may need the verb (changed where necessary for agreement or tense), a noun (singular or plural), an adjective, or an adverb. Sometimes the form may require negative prefixes such as *un-*, *dis-*, or *in-*. For example:

calculate

a. According to the treasurer's <u>calculation</u>, the firm had an increase in profits last year. (*noun form*)

b. Are you able to <u>calculate</u> your income tax by yourself? (*verb form*)

c. A <u>calculating</u> person considers the feelings of other people only if it is to his or her advantage. (*adjective form*)

1. **complain**

   a. The physician examined him last week when he ——————————— about pains in his chest.

   b. A ——————————— about the quality of the product should be directed to the president of the company.

   c. My child is a constant ——————————— about his food, his toys, and his friends.

2. **popular**

   a. Some authors, such as Shakespeare, have maintained their ——————————— for several centuries.

   b. Television is probably the most ——————————— form of entertainment in the world today.

   c. Psychologists believe that movies and television have ——————————— the use of violence.

   d. Abraham Lincoln was ——————————— known as the Great Emancipator.

   e. Do you approve of the ——————————— of the Old Testament in the movies?

3. **compete**

   a. Strong ——————————— among students sometimes leads to cheating.

   b. Children often ——————————— for the affection of their parents.

   c. The two women remained friends even though they were ——————————— for the same job.

   d. It is not easy to remain calm in a ——————————— situation.

4. **immortal**

    a. The philosopher Socrates has been _____ through the writings of Plato.

    b. It is hard for some people to accept the fact that they are _____ and must eventually die.

    c. Should reincarnation be considered a form of _____?

    d. No one is _____, but many people wish they could live forever.

5. **combine**

    a. The _____ of sweet and sour foods is very popular in many cultures.

    b. Only the _____ effort of all countries will maintain peace in the world.

    c. My boss always tries to _____ business and pleasure.

6. **efficient**

    a. Firms often hire experts to improve the _____ of their workers.

    b. In order to be _____, it is necessary to be well organized.

    c. Automobiles that are _____ in their use of gasoline waste energy.

    d. Rosa is able to handle both her job and her housework because she schedules her time _____.

7. **monotony**

    a. The lecturer spoke in such a low _____ that the audience fell asleep.

    b. Jobs that do not require much skill are usually _____.

    c. Some people relieve the _____ of their lives with drugs or alcohol.

8. **substance**

    a. A _____ breakfast may be more important to good nutrition than lunch or dinner.

    b. The heir had to _____ his claim to the money by giving proof of his identity.

    c. Some _____ which are poisonous to one species of animal may not harm another.

9. **depress**

    a. _____ is one of the most widespread illnesses in the United States.

    b. Books that describe violence and torture are very _____ to me.

    c. A person may become _____ after the death of a close relative or friend.

    d. His negative attitude _____ everyone who talks to him.

10. **judge**

    a. The person who is _____ the contest does not know any of the participants.

    b. Lawyers will sometimes have a conference in the _____ chambers before a trial.

    c. We cannot rely on a doctor whose _____ is poor.

11. **prosper**

    a. It requires a great deal of hard work to develop a _____ business.

    b. Even during an economic depression, many people continue to

    _____.

    c. Natural resources greatly contribute to a country's _____.

12. **satisfy**

    a. The student was disappointed to receive a grade of _____ on his report card.

    b. The employees were all _____ with the generous bonus they received at Christmas.

    c. Are you the kind of person that obtains _____ from helping others?

    d. Whatever you cook always _____ me.

    e. It may be difficult to know in advance what will be a _____ occupation.

13. **luxury**

    a. Today we live much more _____ than our ancestors of only one hundred years ago.

    b. Some modern _____ are the washing machine, the air conditioner, and the automobile.

c. We wonder how they could afford such a ———————————— apartment.

14. **starve**

   a. ———————————— is still a major problem in the world.

   b. Some people ———————————— themselves in order to lose weight.

   c. The ———————————— man fell on the ground when he tried to walk.

SYNONYMS

Rewrite each sentence choosing an appropriate synonym from the list below for each underlined word or phrase.

1. approximate	6. wholesome	11. absorbing
2. familiarize	7. sentinel	12. rendered
3. speculate	8. surplus	13. offense
4. perpetual	9. hoard	14. charity
5. monotony	10. hybrid	15. relieve

1. The guard had to stand at his post for twelve hours.

_____

_____

2. Helene hoped that her new job would change the boring sameness of her life.

_____

_____

3. While scientists develop theories about how the world will end naturally, man may settle the question with bombs.

_____

_____

4. *War and Peace* by Tolstoy was so totally interesting to me that I forgot where I was while I read it.

_____

_____

5. Taking long walks helped to lessen his anxiety about his father's illness.

_____

_____

6. Peanut butter, long regarded as "junk" food, has been found by nutrition experts to be very healthful.

_____

_____

7. The tangelo is a crossbred fruit developed from the tangerine and the orange.

_____

_____

8. The builder could only give a fairly accurate estimate of the cost of the house, not an exact one.

_____

_____

9. I was very appreciative of the assistance the stranger gave me.

_____

_____

10. Squirrels save for future use whatever nuts they can find before winter comes.

_____

_____

11. The breaking of a rule that the dog committed was to climb on a chair.

_____

_____

12. There are so many things to acquaint oneself with when starting a new job.

_____

_____

13. It would be better to find work for poor people than to give money to help them.

_____

_____

14. For thousands of men and women, trying to lose weight is a <u>never ending</u> problem.

_____

_____

15. After paying our expenses for the trip, we had a small <u>amount</u> of money <u>left over</u>.

_____

_____

Grammar

NOUN CLAUSES

A noun clause is a clause that functions as a noun in a sentence. For example, compare the subjects (underlined) in these sentences:

a. All the <u>leftovers</u> had to be thrown out.

b. <u>What was left from fixing those generous portions</u> had to be thrown out.

In example *a*, the "simple" subject of the sentence is the noun *leftovers*. In example *b*, however, no single word functions as the subject of "had to be thrown out." Only the entire clause *what was left from fixing those generous portions* tells us what had to be thrown out. In other words, only the entire clause can be the subject.

Here are other examples of noun clauses functioning as subjects:

c. <u>Whatever his son does</u> is all right with Peter.

d. <u>Whoever made the mistake</u> does not matter to me.

e. <u>How fish reproduce</u> always fascinates young children.

Other uses of noun clauses are:

1. As the *object of a verb.*

   EXAMPLE
   He wondered <u>whether he should consider a change of career.</u>

2. As the *object of a preposition.*

   EXAMPLE
   I was concerned about <u>how I would support myself.</u>

In all the examples above, you may have noted that the noun clause begins with an introductory word, such as *what, whatever, whoever, how,* or *whether.* The following are words that can introduce noun clauses:

that	when	whoever
whether	where	whenever
who	why	wherever
what	how	whomever
which	whatever	

Sometimes the introductory word *that* may be omitted in informal speech or writing if the meaning is clear.

EXAMPLES

I thought at first (that) it looked easy.

Soon Sung complained (that) I was taking too long for my lunch.

Should the sentence be of greater length or complexity, however, it would be advisable to include *that* at the beginning of the noun clause for clarity.

In any case, *that* can only be omitted when its noun clause functions as an object, as in the examples above. When the noun clause is the subject of the sentence, *that* must always be included.

EXAMPLES

<u>That I might lose my job</u> did not occur to me.

<u>That taxes can be reduced</u> is the hope of every taxpayer.

GRAMMAR EXERCISES

A. Match the clauses in the first column with those from the second column, and write out the complete sentences. Some clauses may match with more than one ending. In your completed sentence, underline the noun clause and indicate its function. For example, clause 7 and clause E form the sentence:

I was upset by <u>what she said</u>. (*object of preposition* by)

1. Whether I was fired or not
2. I understood
3. What I had done
4. She was to charge the restaurant
5. That life exists on other planets
6. I could see
7. I was upset by
8. I think
9. When the plane leaves
10. Do you know

A. made the women very angry.
B. where they are going.
C. why the extra helpers ate so much.
D. depends on the weather.
E. what she said.
F. that they had no other job.
G. that I did not square with American efficiency.
H. whatever it would cost to clean the dress.
I. did not matter to me.
J. has not yet been proven.

1. _____

2. _____

3. _____

4. _____

5. _____

6. _____

7. _____

8. _____

9. _____

10. _____

B. Make complete sentences by adding noun clauses. Use a different introductory word in each sentence (see list on page 84).

EXAMPLE

Do you obey . . .

The word *whatever* can be used to form the sentence:

Do you obey <u>whatever instructions your parents give you</u>?

1. My friend believes . . .

_____

_____

2. . . . always interests me.

_____

_____

3. A parent should be concerned about . . .

_____

_____

4. It is impossible to forget . . .

_____

_____

5. I have never understood . . .

_____

_____

6. We will never know the true story of . . .

_____

_____

7. . . . is not important.

_____

_____

8. The author explained to the audience . . .

_____

_____

9. . . . is none of your business.

_____

_____

10. We agree with . . .

_____

_____

SCRAMBLED SENTENCES

The phrases in each sentence are not arranged in the right word order. Rearrange each group of words to form a meaningful sentence. This exercise will give you some practice in the positioning of present participial phrases in a sentence. (In some sentences, there may be more than one correct position for the present participial phrase.)

1. walking around the shop, though all was neat, he was quiet, for several minutes afterward, touching this and that.

_____

_____

2. one of the waiters, once while running in the kitchen, on the floor, with dishes and oil sauce, fell down.

_____

_____

3. competing with the clatter of dishes, at that time, and the roar of Broadway outside, an American orchestra played constantly.

_____

_____

4. from four quarters, the place became, to catch trains, with people hurrying, like Grand Central Station.

_____

_____

5. a good deal of juice, in a cup, in cutting grapefruits, could be caught.

_____

_____

6. to anybody, as for melons, without giving cost, they provided much.

_____

_____

7. from fixing those generous portions, thrown out anyhow, what was left, had to be.

_____

_____

8. was fat, everybody, working here.

_____

_____

9. passing along, was so wasteful, through hungry hands, to feed the garbage pail, all that food.

_____

_____

10. a little surplus, for the lean years, a full year, in that local bank account, meant a farmer could store, hoarding it up.

_____

_____

SENTENCE COMBINING

Use conjunctions such as *if, although, though,* or *when* to combine two sentences into one. If you wish to use other conjunctions, feel free to do so.
You may find more than one possibility in many cases.

EXAMPLE

a. He saw me selling a shawl to a lady who had a limousine with a
chauffeur.
b. The big quarrel began.

The big quarrel began <u>when</u> he saw me selling a shawl to a lady who had a
limousine with a chauffeur.

1a. They are willing to pay.
 b. We should charge high.

_____

_____

2a. He never marked the right price in English.
 b. It was a store only for Americans, and no Oriental customers ever
came here.

_____

_____

3a. You don't learn American business methods.
 b. You will never do here.

_____

_____

4a. I did not have the gift for doing this.
 b. I thought at the time it looked easy.

_____

_____

5a. I tried to carry only two things in one hand, water and a plate of soup.
 b. Some of the soup slipped into a red-haired lady's lap.

6a. The Higginses were master and mistress.
 b. They worked harder than I who was the hired man.

7a. It must be done about eleven or twelve in the morning.
 b. The sun was high and hot.

8a. Mr. Higgins remained a farmer just the same.
 b. Commerce and industry took over the neighboring towns year by year, with stores and factories ever on the increase.

9a. You do it only a few hours a day.
 b. Farming is a wholesome pleasure.

10a. The great occasion came.
 b. The hotel had to turn many away.

Writing Assignments

ESSAY TOPICS

Use at least three words from the vocabulary exercises.

1. a. Compare the food of two different countries. Remember that a comparison implies both similarities and differences.

   OR

   b. Taking the food of one particular country, compare the way it is prepared and served in a restaurant with its preparation and service in a private home.

2. Write an argument supporting or opposing the practice of tipping. (See chapter 3 for an outline of an argumentative essay.) You might wish to consider arguments from the point of view of both the tipper and the person receiving the tip. Remember that waiters are not the only people who expect tips.

3. Write an analysis of the working conditions of your job or of the conditions at your college. Do the conditions contribute to the efficient performance of your work or the successful completion of your studies and courses?

4. Write an essay explaining *how* something works. Some possibilities are:
   a. How a particular machine works.
   b. How something is made. For example, in a restaurant, what are the steps in preparing fast food such as fried chicken or hamburgers? Or the steps in an assembly-line manufacture of a product? Or the steps in developing a photograph?
   c. How something is processed. For example, if you work in an office, what happens to an order after it is received? Or what happens to merchandise after it is received in a store?

   Suggested Outline

   A. Introduction: Tell what you are writing about and why it is of interest or of importance (to you, to the firm, to the public). You might wish to start with an incident or experience that would arouse the reader's interest.

   B, C, D. At least three paragraphs explaining the steps involved. Present the information in a logical order. Time is one way of ordering information: what happens first, second, and so forth. Another type of order is by space or location. For example, if a machine has several parts, performing different tasks, you might move from one part to another. Order in an explanation can be achieved in terms of importance. In an office process, you might begin with the least important part and move to the most important.

   E. Conclusion: Your opinion of the procedure or process— whether efficient or not, even whether necessary or not. Another possibility is to make a suggestion which would encourage the reader to explore the topic further.

PROOFREADING

There are 14 errors in the following passage. Find and correct them. Note: Run-ons (comma splices) and misused infinitives each count as one error.

I looked for a job because I had to help my family. My sister said would talk to her sister-in-law, who was the Executive Assistant at Coney Island Hospital. I filed an application for position of Ward Clerk.

I got the job, before I started working, my supervisor told me to be there for one day to familiarize with the work. The first thing I had to do every morning was to prepare the lab slips so that when the tecnicians came to draw blood from the patients, they will know what type of test was need. I had to answer telephone, order supplies, and entered the test results on the charts of the patients.

People were very nice to me, and I enjoyed to work with the patience. My supervisor told me that I was the first clerk did her work so well, however, I was afraid of losing my job. Soon the city didn't have enough money, so I laid off.

CHAPTER 5

The Neighborhood

My building looks like a cemetery because the colors of the walls are black and grey. But the neighborhood is much too noisy for a cemetery. All the neighbors stay outside of their houses in the summer, spring and fall. Most of them like to stand on the corner, drinking beer or smoking cigarettes, and listening to loud music. Even if they are in their houses, they turn on the radio very loud.

From an African student's paper.

READING PASSAGE

About the Author: Mary Antin was a Russian Jew whose father came to the United States alone and then sent for his wife and family. Her first poem was published in the *Boston Herald.*   Her book, *The Promised Land,* was such a great popular success that she spent six years traveling across the United States, lecturing on the spiritual meaning of America.   She married a professor, had one daughter, and spent the rest of her life on a farm, occasionally writing articles for magazines.

To Think About: As you read, try to answer the following questions.   (See page xiii for reading guidelines.)

1. What are two outstanding qualities of Harrison Avenue?
    (Your answers will be paragraph main ideas.)

2. What do you suppose is the reason that most of the doors in the house were usually open?
    (Your answer will be an implication.)

3. Was Mary optimistic or pessimistic about her future?   Give reasons for your opinion.
    (Your answer will be an implication supported by details.)

4. What are at least three sounds that Mary could distinguish after midnight?
    (Your answers will be supporting details.)

5. As Mary sat awake in the middle of the night, she thought, "The silence asks me many questions that I cannot answer."   What might one of these questions be?
    (Your answer will be an implication drawn from the entire reading passage.)

From
THE PROMISED LAND

MARY ANTIN

(*Living in a number of different places when they first came to the United States, Mary Antin and her family finally settled on Dover Street in Boston.*)

Outwardly, Dover Street is a noisy thoroughfare cut through a South End slum. Turn down any street in the slums at random, and call it by whatever name you please; you will observe there the same fashions of life, death, and endurance. Every one of those streets is a rubbish heap of damaged humanity, and it will take a powerful broom and an ocean of soapsuds to clean it out.

Dover Street is intersected, near its eastern end, where we lived, by Harrison Avenue. Harrison is the heart of the South End ghetto, for the greater part of its length, although its northern end belongs to the realm of Chinatown. Its multifarious* business bursts through the narrow shop doors and overruns the basements, the sidewalk, the street itself, in push-carts and open-air stands. Its multitudinous* population bursts through the greasy tenement doors and floods the corridors, the doorsteps, the gutters, the side streets, pushing in and out among the pushcarts all day long and half the night besides.

Rarely as Harrison Avenue is caught asleep, even more rarely is it found clean. Nothing less than a fire or flood would cleanse* this street. A great deal of filthy rubbish is pitched into the street, often through the windows; and what the ashman on his daily round does not remove is left to be trampled to powder, in which form it steals back into the houses from which it was so recently removed.

Our new home consisted of five small rooms up two flights of stairs. In the "parlor" the dingy paper* hung in rags and the plaster fell in chunks. One of the bedrooms was absolutely dark and airtight. The kitchen windows looked out on a dirty court.

The little front bedroom was assigned to me, with only one partner, my

---

multifarious, multitudinous Context clue: the prefix *multi-*, meaning many.

cleanse Before checking the dictionary (you may need an unabridged one for this word), try

to decide from the context whether there is any difference between *cleanse* and *clean*.

paper Wallpaper.

sister Dora. A mouse could not have led a cat much of a chase across this room; still we found space for a narrow bed, a crazy bureau,* and a small table. From the window there was an unobstructed* view of a lumber-yard, beyond which frowned* the blackened walls of a factory. The fence of the lumberyard was gay with theatre posters and illustrated advertisements of tobacco, whiskey, and baby foods. When the window was open, there was a constant clang and whirr of electric cars,* varied by the screech of machinery, the clatter of empty wagons, or the rumble of heavy trucks.

It must not be supposed that I enjoyed any degree of privacy because I had half a room to myself. We were six in the five rooms; we were bound to* be always in each other's way. And as it was within our flat, so it was in the house as a whole. All doors, beginning with the street door, stood open most of the time; or if they were closed, the tenants did not wear out their knuckles knocking for admittance. I could stand at any time in the unswept entrance hall and tell, from an analysis of the medley of sounds and smells that issued from doors ajar,* what was going on in the several flats below. That guttural,* scolding voice, unremittent as the hissing of a steam pipe, is Mrs. Rasnosky. I make a guess that she is chastising the infant Isaac for taking a second lump of sugar in his tea. Spam! Bam! Yes, and she is rubbing in* her objections with the flat of her hand.* That blubbering and moaning, accompanying an elephantine* tread, is fat Mrs. Casey, second floor, home drunk from an afternoon out, in fear of the vengeance of Mr. Casey; to propitiate him she is burning a pan of bacon, as the choking fumes and outrageous sizzling testify. I hear a feeble whining, interrupted by long silences. It is that scabby baby on the third floor, fallen out of bed again, with nobody home to pick him up.

To escape from these various horrors, I ascend to the roof, where bacon and babies and child-beating are not. But there I find two figures in calico wrappers,* with bare red arms akimbo, a basket of wet clothes in front of each, and only one empty clothesline between them. I do not want to be dragged in as a witness in a case of assault and battery, so I descend to the street again, grateful to note, as I pass, that the third-floor baby is still.

---

a crazy bureau   A used, broken bureau in which the drawers don't fit right.

unobstructed   Context clues: the prefix *un-*, meaning not; base word is *obstruct*.

frowned   Is this a literal use of the word? In what way would walls that frown look like people that frown?

electric cars   Trolley cars, street cars.

bound to   Sure to, certain to.

ajar   Context clue: "All doors . . . stood open most of the time."

guttural   Context clue: From the meaning of the passage, could the word have a pleasant meaning?

rubbing in   Emphasizing.

the flat of her hand   The palm of her hand with the fingers held open.

elephantine   Context clues: base word is *elephant*; the suffix *-ine*, meaning like, similar to.

wrappers   A more modern term would be *housecoat*.

In front of the door I squeeze through a group of children. They are going to play tag and are counting to see who should be "it":

My-mother-and-your-mother-went-out-to-hang-clothes;
My-mother-gave-your-mother-a-punch-in-the-nose.

If the children's couplet does not give a vivid picture of the life, manners, and customs of Dover Street, no description of mine can ever do so.

I was not unhappy on Dover Street; quite the contrary. Everything of consequence was well with me. Poverty was a superficial, temporary matter; it vanished at the touch of money. Money in America was plentiful; it was only a matter of getting some of it, and I was on my way to the mint. If Dover Street was not a pleasant place to abide in, it was only a wayside* house. And I was really happy, actively happy, in the exercise of my mind in Latin, mathematics, history, and the rest, the things that suffice* a studious girl in the middle teens.

Still I had moments of depression, when my whole being protested against the life of the slum. I resented the familiarity of my vulgar neighbors. I felt myself defiled by the indecencies I was compelled to witness. Then it was I took to running away from home. I went out in the twilight

---

wayside Context clue: the meaning of each half of the word, taking the second half first.

suffice Context clue: This is a verb (subject is "that") related to *sufficient*.

and walked for hours, my blind* feet leading me. I did not care where I went. If I lost my way, so much the better; I never wanted to see Dover Street again.

But behold, as I left the crowds behind and the broader avenues were spanned by the open sky, my grievances melted away, and I fell to dreaming of things that neither hurt nor pleased. A fringe of trees against the sunset became suddenly the symbol of the whole world, and I stood and gazed. The sunset faded; the trees withdrew.

A favorite resort of mine, after dark, was the South Boston Bridge, across South Bay and the Old Colony Railroad. This was so near home that I could go there at any time when the confusion in the house drove me out, or I felt the need of fresh air. I liked to stand leaning on the bridge railing and look down on the dim tangle of railroad tracks below. I could barely see them branching out, elbowing,* winding, and sliding out into the night in pairs. I was fascinated by the dotted lights, the significant red and green of signal lamps. These simple things stood for a complexity that it made me dizzy to think of. Then the blackness below me was split by the fiery eye of a monster engine,* his breath enveloped* me in blinding clouds, his long body shot by, rattling a hundred claws of steel, and he was gone, with an imperative shriek that shook me where I stood.

So would I be, swift on my rightful business, picking out my proper track from the million that cross it, pausing for no obstacles, sure of my goal.

After my watches on the bridge I often stayed up to write or study. It is late before Dover Street begins to go to bed. It is past midnight before I feel that I am alone. Seated in my stiff little chair before my narrow table, I gather in the night sounds through the open window, curious to assort and define them. As little by little, the city settles down to sleep, the volume of sound diminishes, and the qualities of particular sounds stand out. The electric car lurches by with silent gong, taking the empty track by leaps, humming to itself in the invisible distance. A few pedestrians hurry by, their heavy boots all out of step. The distant thoroughfares have long ago ceased their murmur, and I know that a million lamps shine idly in the idle street.

My sister sleeps quietly in the little bed. The rhythmic dripping of a faucet is audible through the flat. It is so still that I can hear the paper crackling on the wall. Silence upon silence is added to the night; only the kitchen clock is the voice of my brooding thoughts—ticking, ticking, ticking.

Suddenly the distant whistle of a locomotive breaks the stillness with a long-drawn* wail. Like a threatened trouble, the sound comes nearer,

---

blind   In what way could feet be blind?

elbowing   Is this a literal use of the word?

monster engine   Notice all the words that are used to make the engine seem like an animal.

enveloped   Context clues: This is a past-tense verb (subject is "breath"); base word is envelope.

long-drawn   Continued for a long time.

piercingly near; then it dies out in a mangled silence, complaining to the last.

The sleepers stir in their beds. Somebody sighs, and the burden of all his trouble falls upon my heart. A homeless cat cries in the alley, in the voice of a human child. And the ticking of the kitchen clock is the voice of my troubled thoughts.

Many things are revealed to me as I sit and watch the world sleep. But the silence asks me many questions that I cannot answer; I am glad when the tide of sound begins to return, little by little, and I welcome the clatter of tin cans that announces the milkman. I cannot see him in the dusk, but I know his wholesome face has no problem in it.

It is one flight up to the roof; it is a leap of the soul to the sunrise. The morning mist rests lightly on chimneys and roofs and walls, wreathes the lamp-posts, and floats in gauzy streamers down the streets. Distant buildings are massed like palace walls, with turrets and spires* lost in the rosy clouds. I love my beautiful city spreading all about me. I love the world. I love my place in the world.

---

turrets and spires   Context clue: ''lost in the
rosy clouds.''

Comprehension

These questions are to be answered orally or in writing. Some of them may require more than one sentence for your answer.

1. Did Mary Antin live near or far from the heart of the South End ghetto? Explain your answer.
2. What are two outstanding qualities of Harrison Avenue?
3. Did every room in Mary's apartment have a window? How do you know?
4. Why does the author put the word "parlor" in quotation marks?
5. What do you suppose is the reason that most of the doors in the house were usually open?
6. Did tenants bother to knock when they wanted to visit each other?
7. Why was Mrs. Casey afraid of her husband?
8. Do you think Mr. Casey was satisfied with the bacon Mrs. Casey prepared? Why?
9. What does Mary mean when she says she does not want to be dragged in as a witness in a case of assault and battery?
10. Was Mary optimistic or pessimistic about her future? Give reasons for your opinion.
11. Why does Mary call her feet "blind"?
12. In what way did the trees withdraw when the sunset faded? Did they go away?
13. Why did Mary like to go to the South Boston Bridge?
14. Why are the red and green railroad signal lights significant?
15. How does the author compare herself to the "monster engine"?
16. What are at least three sounds that Mary could distinguish after midnight?
17. As Mary sat awake in the middle of the night, she thought, "The silence asks me many questions that I cannot answer." What might one of these questions be?

DISCUSSION QUESTIONS

1. Is there an area in your city that is considered a ghetto? Does one particular race or ethnic group live there? Is it necessary for a neighborhood to be poor to be considered a ghetto? What are the characteristics of a ghetto? Have you experienced life in a ghetto? How does it compare with Antin's description?
2. Where can one find pushcarts or open-air stands in your city or town?

What is sold on these carts or stands? Have you noticed any motor vehicles which now take the place of the old pushcarts?

3. Do you ever feel the need to get away from your home or your neighborhood? What causes your feeling? Where do you go or what do you do when you want to escape your surroundings?

4. Mary Antin seems to feel that her living conditions were bad because there were six people living in five small rooms and she shared a tiny room with her sister. Do you consider this crowded? Under what conditions have you lived? What do you consider ideal living conditions?

5. A number of details in the reading passage indicate that the events took place many years ago (actually just before the year 1900). For example, in most cities, milk is no longer usually delivered in tin cans, but in bottles (or in plastic cartons to the stores). Discuss similar details that have changed over the years.

CLOZE EXERCISE

Fill in each blank with a single (one) word.

Still I had moments _____ depression, when my whole

_____ protested against the life _____ the slum. I re-

sented _____ familiarity of my vulgar _____. I felt myself

defiled _____ the indecencies I was _____ to witness.

Then it _____ I took to running _____ from home. I

went _____ in the twilight and _____ for hours, my

blind _____ leading me. I did _____ care where I

went. _____ I lost my way, _____ much the better;

I _____ wanted to see Dover Street _____.

Vocabulary

Fill in the blanks with the correct forms of the word given for each group of sentences. You may need a verb (changed where necessary for agreement or tense), a noun (singular or plural), an adjective, or an adverb. For example:

endure

a. In a crisis, one has to <u>endure</u> all the hardships encountered. (*verb*)

b. The physical education teacher gave a test of <u>endurance</u> to all the participants in the game. (*noun*)

c. As one grows older, it is difficult to form <u>enduring</u> relationships. (*adjective*)

1. **damage**

   a. After the typhoon, everything in the town was _____.

   b. His opponent in the election made a _____ remark about his private life.

   c. A lot of _____ was caused by the explosion of a bomb hidden in one of the lockers.

2. **intersect**

   a. One has to be extra careful when driving through an _____.

   b. The street where they live happens to _____ with the railroad track.

   c. On one end Park Avenue is _____ by 37th Street.

3. **obstruct**

   a. That tall gentleman standing in front _____ the view of the game.

   b. During the parade, the scene was _____ by a photographer taking pictures.

   c. The doctors gave him a series of tests to see if there was any

   _____ in the intestines.

4. **complex**

   a. The psychologist told her that her problem was very _____.

   b. A committee was formed to study the _____ of the issue.

c. The jury could not come to a decision because the case was too

_____.

d. Her mother died because she developed _____ in her illness.

5. **illustrate**

a. Please _____ your statement with examples.

b. The artist was asked to give an _____ of her work.

c. Her designs were _____ in the fashion magazine.

6. **vary**

a. _____ people attended the International Conference in Science.

b. The Christmas season brings a _____ of presents for the children.

c. The sad expression on her face never _____.

d. This machine produces _____ degrees of heat.

7. **admit**

a. The price of _____ to the play was too high for the students.

b. He was allowed _____ into the surgery room to witness an operation.

c. The hospital only _____ visitors at certain hours of the day.

8. **analyze**

a. In order to find the solution, one has to _____ the problem carefully.

b. An _____ mind is necessary to understand philosophy.

c. The students were told to write out the _____ of the experiment.

9. **object**

a. I have no _____ to your joining the army.

b. Her father _____ to her seeing this boy from the South.

c. Is it possible to be _____ about oneself?

d. He discussed the issue with _____.

10. **accompany**

a. On his trip to Europe, he was _____ by his mother.

b. Would you like to ———————————— me to see the show?

c. During the recital, she played the piano without any ————————————.

11. **consequent**

a. Poverty was the ———————————— of his actions.

b. The senator exposed the corruption of the big oil companies; ————————————, they were asked to reorganize on the executive level.

c. If we add the soy sauce, the ———————————— taste will be sharper.

12. **compel**

a. Young teachers feel ———————————— to prove their own expertise.

b. The ———————————— situation forced the police to break down the door.

c. Teachers ———————————— students to do their homework.

13. **resent**

a. College students are ———————————— when forced to take certain courses.

b. There is a lot of ———————————— among young people today concerning parental supervision.

c. I ———————————— his calling me a liar.

14. **employ**

a. The New York Telephone Company ———————————— thousands of workers.

b. He has been collecting ———————————— checks since he lost his job.

c. Many college graduates find it difficult to seek ———————————— in different professions.

d. There are few ———————————— who give an annual bonus.

e. One of the ———————————— who worked in the construction of that building died from an accident.

15. **respond**

a. I did not receive any ———————————— after she left for Chicago.

b. Did you ———————————— to the invitation given by the president of the college?

c. The women's liberation movement is ———————————— to some of the needs of working mothers. (Use the adjective form.)

d. His patient is not ———————————— to the medication given to her.

SYNONYMS

Rewrite each sentence choosing an appropriate synonym from the list below for each underlined word or phrase.

1. vulgar	6. greasy	11. filthy
2. confusion	7. assault	12. grievance
3. burst	8. multitudinous	13. consequence
4. propitiate	9. fascinated	14. diminished
5. ascend	10. outrageous	15. testify

1. A large crowd <u>emerged suddenly</u> on the scene of the robbery.

_____

_____

2. Clean <u>oily</u> pans after you are through cooking.

_____

_____

3. The latest typhoon in Asia affected <u>numerous</u> inhabitants.

_____

_____

4. He left his neighborhood because the place was <u>very dirty</u>.

_____

_____

5. John does not know how to <u>appease</u> his father's anger.

_____

_____

6. The police department advises the community to report any case of <u>a violent attack</u>.

_____

_____

7. It was <u>totally disgraceful</u> that he acted so childishly in front of the whole class.

_____

_____

8. Mary has to <u>walk up</u> to the top floor in order to get to the other building.

_____

_____

9. A group of laid-off employees filed a <u>complaint</u> through the labor union.

_____

_____

10. Her strict parents make sure that she does not go out with <u>ignorant and uncultivated</u> people.

_____

_____

11. He was imprisoned as a <u>result</u> of his illegal transactions with foreign businessmen.

_____

_____

12. To some outsiders, the Cultural Revolution in China caused total <u>disorder</u> among the people.

_____

_____

13. Foreign visitors are <u>strongly attracted</u> by the skyscrapers in New York City.

_____

_____

14. As the wind <u>lessened</u>, the rain also decreased.

_____

_____

15. The witness refused to <u>give evidence</u> at the trial.

_____

_____

Grammar

PREPOSITIONS

Many idioms combine common verbs with prepositions.

EXAMPLES

Nobody knew what <u>was going on</u>.
verb + preposition

The bus driver told him when <u>to get off</u>.
verb + preposition
(infinitive)

In each case, the preposition is needed to complete the particular idiomatic meaning of the verb.

Another common use of prepositions is to introduce phrases.

EXAMPLE

Joanne changed the flat tire <u>in ten minutes</u>.
prepositional phrase

These two common uses of prepositions—following a verb and in a prepositional phrase—may be confusing when combined together.

EXAMPLES

Nobody knew what was going <u>on</u> <u>in</u> the classroom.

The driver told him to get <u>off</u> <u>before</u> the other passengers.

He passed <u>out</u> <u>from</u> the heat.

The arrows show which preposition belongs to the verb and which belongs to the prepositional phrase. Note that both prepositions are needed in each sentence.

GRAMMAR EXERCISES

A. Underline the prepositions and use arrows (as above) to indicate whether they belong to the verbs or to the prepositional phrases.

1. The weather cleared up at five o'clock.

2. Please drop in for a chat.

3. They walked by in a hurry.

4. I did not want to be dragged in as a witness.

5. The people push in and out among the pushcarts.

B. In each of the following sentences, a preposition has been omitted. In some cases, it is the one that belongs to the verb: in others, it is the one introducing the prepositional phrase. Insert the missing preposition in the proper place.

EXAMPLE

My sister will put you up $\overset{\text{for}}{\wedge}$ the night.

1. Please do that over the morning.

2. I hope you will drop for a chat the next time you are in my neighborhood.

3. He always puts his toys away the shelf.

4. They ran away another city.

5. The dog was run by a bus.

6. The sound dies out a mangled silence.

7. She is a person you can reason in a calm manner.

8. The lights were turned off the whole building.

9. He was brought up his grandmother.

10. The fire has been put out the fourth floor.

C. Write complete sentences using a verb-preposition combination from the first column together with a prepositional phrase from the second column. Change the verb forms for agreement and tense where necessary.
For example, combine 1, <u>call up</u>, with D, <u>by 3 P.M.</u>, to form:

I will call you up by 3 P.M.

1. call up	A. for an hour
2. come in	B. in his struggle
3. wake up	C. on the road
4. go out	D. by 3 P.M.
5. pass by	E. in a hurry
6. get up	F. in another direction
7. give up	G. with a friend
8. look away	H. in London
9. grow up	I. at 10 A.M.

1. _____

2. _____

3. _____

4. _____

5. _____

6. _____

7. _____

8. _____

9. _____

SCRAMBLED SENTENCES

The phrases in each sentence are not arranged in the right word order. Rearrange each group of words to form a meaningful sentence. This exercise will give you some practice in the positioning of prepositions which follow verbs.

1. a pleasant place, Dover Place, in, not, to abide, was.

_____

_____

2. leaning, to stand, the bridge railing, I like, on,

_____

_____

3. I squeeze, in front, of children, of the door, through a group.

_____

_____

4. from these various horrors, to the roof, I ascend, to escape.

_____

_____

5. with the flat, she is, in her objections, of her hand, rubbing.

_____

_____

6. through, its multifarious business, the narrow shop doors, bursts.

_____

_____

7. of five small rooms, our new home, two flights of stairs, up, consisted.

_____

_____

8. out their knuckles, the tenants, did not wear, for admittance, knocking.

_____

_____

9. to clean it, it will take, and, out, of soapsuds, a powerful broom, an ocean.

_____

_____

10. from the smells, from the doors, down below, I could tell, on, that issued, what was going.

_____

_____

SENTENCE COMBINING

Use conjunctions such as *before, after,* and *because* to combine two sentences into one. If you wish to use other conjunctions, feel free to do so. You may find more than one possibility in many cases.

EXAMPLE
a. The athlete lost the game.
b. He played badly.
The athlete lost the game <u>because</u> he played badly.

1a. He searched for a week.
 b. He came up with an answer.

_____

_____

2a. Frieda was married to John.
 b. We came to East Boston.

_____

_____

3a. I believed that America was not going to provide everything for my family.
b. I started to think of ways and means of getting rich.

_____

_____

4a. John did his income-tax return.
b. He had to read carefully the rules stated in the tax guide.

_____

_____

5a. She heard the news about the death of her father.
b. She went into a coma.

_____

_____

6a. John is very careful in choosing his partners.
b. He wants to make sure that his plans will work out smoothly.

_____

_____

7a. Robert watches the scene across the river at night.
b. He often stays up to write about the scene.

_____

_____

8a. We started the trip.
b. We were held up for three or four days with engine trouble.

_____

_____

9a. I waited for half an hour at the doctor's office.
b. The doctor had an emergency call.

_____

_____

10a. John was not happy.
b. The hotel looked extremely expensive.

_____

_____

Writing Assignments

ESSAY TOPICS

Use at least three words from the vocabulary exercises.

1. Compare children's games of two different countries.
2. Describe the living conditions that you would consider ideal. Include the country, the type and size of the city or town, the neighborhood in which you would prefer to live, and the kind of house or apartment you would like to have.
3. Write an argument in favor of or in opposition to ethnic neighborhoods. Unlike ghettos, which are poor slum areas, many working-class or middle-class neighborhoods consist of one minority or ethnic group. Your argument should show the advantages or disadvantages of living in such ethnic neighborhoods.
4. A *ghetto* is defined in the dictionary as a "slum section of a city occupied predominantly by members of a minority group who live there because of social or economic pressure." Keeping a particular ethnic or minority ghetto in mind, write a paper in which you expand the definition of *ghetto*. Give your definition essay a thesis (main idea) such as "It is impossible to escape from a ghetto" or "Ghetto life provides motivation for success." You can see that your particular definition of a ghetto will depend on the point of view you express in your thesis.

   Suggested Outline
   - A. Introduction: Explain what kind of ghetto you are writing about and introduce your main idea or thesis. You might wish to use an experience or incident to lead into your thesis.
   - B, C, D. At least three paragraphs supporting your view or definition of a ghetto. You can use more than one pattern of composition in developing your paper. You might:
     Compare and contrast the ghetto with other neighborhoods.
     Discuss the causes, such as the attitude of society, which contributed to form the ghetto.
     Discuss the effects of living in the ghetto on individuals.
     Give examples of experiences and incidents.
     Give arguments for your thesis.
   - E. Conclusion: There are many possibilities. One might be your opinion of whether ghettos should, or can, be eliminated.

PROOFREADING

There are 15 errors in the following passage. Find and correct them. Note: Misused infinitives each count as one error.

I live in the west side of Manhattan. Cross the street from my house

is the junior high school that I use to attend. On the block, there are many old buldings that seem to be falling down. There is also a super-market, a barbar shop, three restaurants, a Chinese laundry, and a fire-house. During daytime, the street is filled with children from the school. At night, many rich, high-class people drive around in their big Cadillacs and Mercedes-Benzes and looking for parking spaces. That is because they are going to all the theaters and playhouses that are locate in the area. I like the neighborhood, but I am little ashame to tell people where I live. Everyone know that the area is full of prostitute. Although I don't mind to live here right now, but I wouldn't want to stay here forever.

CHAPTER 6

Cultural Conflicts

Puerto Rican dishes are principally made up of rice, beans, and meat; it takes about 45 minutes to prepare this popular meal.   Since I do not like to wait so long when I am hungry, I usually eat American foods such as canned vegetables, hamburgers, and hot dogs.

From a Puerto Rican student's paper.

READING PASSAGE

About the Author: Chin Y. Lee was born in China, where he received his B.A.   He lived in Burma, Indochina, and India before coming to the United States to study for his M.A. in drama at Yale University.   He has worked as an editor for two Chinese-language newspapers in San Francisco and also served as a writer for Radio Free Asia.   *Flower Drum Song*, his first novel, later became a play on Broadway as well as a Hollywood movie.

To Think About: As you read, try to answer the following questions.   (See page xiii for reading guidelines.)

1. What did Westernizing the household mean to Wang San?
   (Your answer will be the main idea of the paragraph.)

2. What made Old Master Wang think that his son really knew his lessons?
   (Your answer will be an implication.)

3. In what way did Wang Ta and Mr. Loo's second daughter prove to be very much alike?
   (Your answer will be an implication.)

4. Summarize the conflicts between Master Wang and his sons.
   (Your answer will be the main ideas of the reading passage.)

From
FLOWER DRUM SONG

C. Y. LEE

(In this novel, Old Master Wang tries to maintain the Chinese culture and tradition that he brought with him to the United States. He is strongly resisted by his sons, Wang San and Wang Ta, who have become Americanized. In this passage, Wang San has the mistaken impression that his father is going to Westernize the household.)

Wang San had no school today. But he hated Saturdays and Sundays because he had to eat all his meals at home. Whenever he saw the typical Hunan dishes, he lost his appetite. Sometimes he would sneak out and eat a hot dog or a hamburger before meals. If he had no money, he would raid the icebox* when the cook wasn't in the kitchen. When he was very hungry, he would raid it anyway, cook or no cook. Usually he was the hungriest when the family dinner was the richest, for there were so many delicacies on the table that Wang San hated. The only food he enjoyed at home was the raw Chinese ham in the icebox.

Now that he had learned his father was going to Westernize* the household, he was excited. There were a lot of things he would like to do at home but had never dared, such as reading comic books on the living-room floor, chewing bubble gum, shooting birds in the backyard with an air gun, and so on. Now perhaps he could do all these things without arousing his father's anger.

At lunch time he boldly brought home a loaf of bread. Instead of eating rice he made sandwiches with the Chinese dishes. While he was enjoying his sandwiches, his father looked at him with a deep scowl. "What kind of food is that?" Old Master Wang asked.

"Sandwiches, father," Wang San said.

"What a barbarous way of eating it," his father said. "Use your chopsticks!"

"You are not supposed to eat a sandwich with chopsticks, father. This is American food."

"What is wrong with the Chinese food on this table?"

---

raid the icebox   Take things from the icebox that one is not supposed to.

Westernize   Context clues: This is a verb; base word is *West*. The United States is considered a Western country as opposed to the Eastern ones such as China or Japan.

"I like American food better."

Old Master Wang's scowl became deeper.

"Did you study this morning?"

"Yes, father."

"Come to my room and recite your lessons to me after lunch," Old Master Wang said, rising. Wang San's sandwich and table manners had ruined his appetite. He couldn't eat any more.

After his father had left the table, Wang San enjoyed his sandwich even more. He didn't know that the Chinese dishes, which he had disliked, could taste so good with bread. He was glad that his father hadn't said anything about forbidding him to eat sandwiches.

Although the recitation routine was nothing difficult, for his father didn't understand a word of what he was reciting anyway, it was annoying and often made him nervous. He took his schoolbooks and went to his father's room. "What lessons have you studied this morning?" Old Master Wang asked, groaning and clearing his throat.

"Geography and arithmetic," Wang San said.

"Put your books down," his father said.

Wang San laid his books on the desk and waited. "Which lesson of geography have you studied?" his father asked.

"Lesson nine."

"Recite lesson nine."

Wang San recited lesson nine about North America, and when he began to stammer, he quickly switched to the American Declaration of Independence, which he had memorized and could recite fluently. When Wang San finished, Old Master Wang nodded his head with approval and grunted, "Hm, not bad, not bad. Which lesson of arithmetic have you studied?"

"Lesson ten," Wang San said.

"Recite lesson ten."

Wang San didn't argue that arithmetic lessons were not to be recited. He knew his father, who believed that anything a student learned at school must be memorized. It was the system practiced in China for thousands of years, and Old Master Wang firmly believed it was the only system that could help the student learn anything. "Lesson ten, go on," he said.

Wang San cleared his voice and repeated the American Declaration of Independence, twice this time. When he finished, he shifted his legs restlessly and waited anxiously for his father to dismiss him. He didn't want to be late for the ball game. He was getting more uncomfortable now. Old Master Wang coughed and asked, "Is that all?"

"Yes."

"Next time study more."

"Yes, father. May I go now?"

Old Master Wang looked at his son sternly and asked, "Why are you so anxious to go?"

"M-my aunt wants me to visit her," Wang San said.

Old Master Wang couldn't object to his sons' going to their aunt's for fear he might displease his sister-in-law, who had insisted that relatives should visit each other as often as possible. But he didn't let Wang San go until after he had given him a lecture on manners, honesty and filial piety.

After Wang San had left, Old Master Wang decided to take a walk in Chinatown. As he was going down the hill and passing the Chinese playground, he suddenly saw Wang San throwing a leather ball over a net with a group of youngsters. He blinked a few times to make sure it was his son. Yes, it was he. Was that how he visited his aunt?

Old Master Wang felt anger rising in him. He hated his son's dishonesty, especially after he had just lectured him on the subject of honesty. He controlled a strong desire to go over to his son and box his ear for lying. He coughed to attract his son's attention, but Wang San was so engrossed* in the game he never noticed his father. Old Master Wang's anger was rising fast as he watched his son, but soon he was amazed at Wang San's skill in hitting the leather ball.

On his way home, he realized that Wang San's hands must have been toughened by this game. No wonder the boy had become less afraid of his bamboo stick. Next time he punished him, he must hit harder.

(*Wang Ta, the older son, has found a girl he wants to marry. Before he can even mention the idea, his father decides to arrange for his marriage in the traditional way.*)

Old Master Wang cleared his throat. "My son, Confucius has said, 'There are three major offenses to the ancestors; lack of descendants is the worst.' Now you are almost thirty, it is time for you to take a wife."

Wang Ta was somewhat surprised, for that was exactly what he had planned to talk to his father about. "I have thought of that, father. I am happy to say I have finally found the right girl whom I . . ."

"Finding the right woman is not your business," Old Master Wang said bluntly. "That responsibility rests on the shoulders of the parents who are more experienced in this matter."

"Do you mean—do you mean you have already chosen a wife for me?" Wang Ta asked.

"Yes, we have," Old Master Wang said, his voice softened, and there was almost a smile on his face. "Your aunt and I have found the right woman for you."

Wang Ta managed to control his rising anger; he paused for a moment before he spoke. "Father, I shall try to stand your telling me what to eat and what to wear, for I can spit out the food I do not like, and I can change the clothes that do not fit me. But a wife is like a man's shadow; if you do not mind, I would like to choose her myself."

"You young people are never careful," Old Master Wang said, displeased, but trying his best to keep the conversation pleasant. "I have seen the younger generation change their wives more often than they change their clothes. That is why the parents must make the choice."

---

engrossed   Context clue: the meaning of the sentence.

"Father, this is the only thing I shall not tolerate. Our points of view are different; probably they are thousands of miles apart. No, I would rather die as a lonely bachelor than be tied down to a dumb, ugly old strange woman."

"She is not dumb, ugly or old," Old Master Wang interrupted him hotly. "She is the second daughter of Old Mr. Loo, a good friend of your aunt's, a poet and a scholar, highly regarded in Chinatown for his scholastic achievement . . ."

"You see, father, our points of view are so different. You talk as though it was the father, not the daughter, whom I am supposed to marry. Father, I might as well tell you the truth. I have already found . . ."

Old Master Wang shot up to his feet and said angrily, "I have already engaged you to Old Mr. Loo's second daughter, and Mr. Loo has agreed to marry her ahead of her older sister. That is a big face* he has bestowed upon us. You are going to marry her on the fifth of the fourth moon. That is a lucky date chosen by Mr. Foon, the leading physiognomist in Chinatown."

Wang Ta was stunned for a moment. He would never have antagonized*

---

a big face An honor.

antagonized Context clue: related to "boldly."

his father so boldly if he had not been in love. Now that his own marriage plans faced the threat of being wrecked, he surprised himself by being more bold.

"Father," he said, starting for the door, "I am not going to marry anyone on the fifth of the fourth moon. I advise you to worry more about your own cough than my marriage!" He went out of the house, slamming the front door.

"Oh, rebellious dog," Old Master Wang said furiously without losing his dignity. He paced the floor trying to control his rage. "Ah, the younger generation," he mumbled to himself. "Rebellious! Outrageous! They have no manners, no respect for their elders! Some day they will have the gall* to cut their own father's throat!"

(Later, Master Wang hears some news from his sister-in-law, Madam Tang.)

"My sister's husband," Madam Tang said the moment Old Master Wang had stepped into the hall, "please tell your maid to go to the house of Loo and bring the two geese back."

Old Master Wang was shocked for a moment. "What do you mean?" he asked.

"Mr. Loo's second daughter just rebelled," Madam Tang said. "She just told her father that she is already secretly engaged to a white American. They are going to get married immediately. Her father tried to forbid the marriage, but the girl said that she is over twenty-one and she can marry anyone she wishes."

Old Master Wang grunted. Somehow he felt slightly relieved, for the prospect of taming Wang Ta and making him accept the girl had been a burden on his mind.

"Besides," Madam Tang said, fanning herself with her handkerchief rapidly, "that girl has been insulting. She said that even if she was not engaged, she would not allow herself to be thrown at anybody in town. Her father told her that Wang Ta is from a wealthy family. Do you know what that girl said? She said in that case Wang Ta must be a good-for-nothing playboy* whose only use in the world is to turn food into manure. Just imagine a young girl saying such a thing!"

Old Master Wang cleared his throat. "What did I tell you, my wife's sister?" he said. "The younger generation is all spoiled. However, I am glad that this girl has objected to this marriage. My dog son, Wang Ta, has just refused to marry her too."

"Has he?" Madam Tang said, her face brightening; then she triumphantly brought her palm down on the low table and added, "He has done the right thing! We must let that vulgar girl know that she was turned down first!"

"Oh, what difference does it make now?" Old Master Wang said.

---

gall Context clue: related to "no manners," "no respect."

playboy Context clues: base words are *play* and *boy*; also, the meaning of the sentence.

"One crow* is not darker than the other. Both are spoiled eggs* of the modern times."

"My sister's husband, after I heard what that vulgar girl just said to her father, I began to realize that Wang Ta is a hundred times more cultured than she is. I just pity that white American man who is going to marry her. Now, even if she crawls to this house and begs you to take her, I would advise you to kick her out with both your feet!"

Old Master Wang grunted. "Tell you the truth, a moment ago I almost had a good mind to kick Wang Ta out and disown* that unfilial dog."

"All right," Madam Tang said, "let bygones be bygones. Fortunately no servants know of this unpleasant experience. If anybody knows, we must see to it that he does not gossip about it in Chinatown." Suddenly she spotted Wang San in the corner; she pointed a finger at him and asked, "What is the meaning of that?"

"I am giving that little devil some standing punishment."

"What crime did he commit this time? Did he steal again?"

"No; laziness, an offense worse than theft."

"He has just reached the lazy age. It is natural, my sister's husband; nobody can help it. Please let him go. I hate to see my sister's own flesh and blood suffer this stiff, uncomfortable posture. My sister's husband, do not forget that we are living in a modern world."

"My wife's sister, by your customs, you seem to belong to the modern generation; but by your age, you can not deny that you are still a member of the old. Please tell me honestly, have you not missed the good old days? Those days when children were respectful and obedient, virtues were high, life was serene and peaceful. . . ."

Madam Tang liked the good old days in China, but she also found many new comforts in the modern world. To her a combination of the old and new would be ideal.

---

crow; spoiled eggs These are metaphorical expressions (see page 36).

disown Context clue: the prefix *dis-*, meaning not.

Comprehension

These questions are to be answered orally or in writing. Some of them may require more than one sentence for your answer.

1. What did Westernizing the household mean to Wang San?
2. Why was old Master Wang upset at lunchtime?
3. What was unusual about the fact that Wang San recited his lessons to his father?
4. What made Old Master Wang think that his son really knew his lessons?
5. Master Wang gave Wang San a lecture on manners, honesty, and filial piety. Even in the short passage up to this point, what proves that Wang San did not practice at least two of these virtues?
6. Why did Master Wang resolve to hit his son harder the next time he punished him?
7. What did Wang Ta mean when he said that he wanted to choose his wife himself because a wife is like a man's shadow?
8. How did Wang Ta differ from his father in evaluating the qualities of a good wife?
9. According to Master Wang, how had Mr. Loo honored the family in agreeing to marry his second daughter to Wang Ta?
10. In what way did Wang Ta and Mr. Loo's second daughter prove to be very much alike?
11. What was Master Wang's reaction to the news that Mr. Loo's daughter refused to marry Wang Ta?
12. What particularly upset Madam Tang in the refusal by Mr. Loo's daughter to marry Wang Ta?
13. What did Master Wang mean when he said that one crow is not darker than the other?
14. How did Master Wang and Madam Tang differ in their attitudes toward "the good old days"?
15. Summarize the conflicts between Master Wang and his sons.

DISCUSSION QUESTIONS

1. Have your food preferences changed or remained the same since you came to this country? Do you have arguments with your parents about the food they serve and the food you prefer to eat? Does your family have difficulty in obtaining your native foods here?
2. What are some differences between the teaching methods and classroom

practices of your own country and those here? Where do you think it is easier to learn?

3. What conflicts do you have with your parents about friends, dating, or marriage? Do they want to control whom you go out with? Do they expect to arrange your marriage? Are differences with your parents caused by cultural customs or simply by the usual "generation gap"?

4. What customs of your own country did you have to give up when you came here? Do you find any difference in the respect shown for parents in the two cultures? Which new customs were you glad to adopt, and which have given you difficulty?

5. Unlike most of the other reading passages in this book, which are autobiographical and, therefore, based on an actual person's life, this chapter's passage was taken from a novel—a work of fiction. Do you notice any difference between the two kinds of readings? Does this one seem less real, less true to life, or just as realistic as the others?

CLOZE EXERCISE

Fill in each blank with a single (one) word.

Wang San recited lesson nine _____ North America, and when he _____ to stammer, he quickly switched _____ the American Declaration of Independence, _____ he had memorized and could _____ fluently. When Wang San finished, _____ Master Wang nodded his head _____ approval and grunted, "Hm, not _____, not bad. Which lesson _____ arithmetic have you studied?"

Wang San didn't argue _____ arithmetic lessons were not _____ be recited. He knew _____ father, who believed that _____ a student learned at _____ must be memorized. It _____ the system practiced in _____ for thousands of years, _____ Old Master Wang firmly _____ it was the only _____ that could help the _____ learn anything. "Lesson ten, _____ on," he said.

Wang San cleared his voice _____ repeated the American Declaration of _____, twice this time. When he _____, he shifted his legs restlessly _____ waited anxiously for his father

_____ dismiss him. He didn't want to _____ late for the ball _____. He was getting more uncomfortable _____.

Old Master Wang coughed and _____, "Is that all?"

Vocabulary

WORD FORMS

Fill in the blanks with the correct forms of the word given for each group of sentences. You may need the verb (changed where necessary for agreement or tense), participles, a noun (singular or plural), an adjective, or an adverb. Sometimes the form may require negative prefixes such as *un-*, *dis-*, or *in-*. For example:

ruin
   a. My friends visited the Egyptian <u>ruins</u> during their stay there. (*noun form*)
   b. The insect spray is <u>ruining</u> my plants. (*verb form*)
   c. My sister <u>ruined</u> my party dress when she ironed it. (*verb form*)

1. **excite**

   a. Luce _____ her parents to anger.

   b. Their trip on the safari in Africa was very _____.

   c. The shooting at the amusement park created some _____ among the audience.

   d. Since he is very tense, an argument _____ him easily.

2. **punish**

   a. Capital _____ was accepted as a law in many states.

   b. His acts of child abuse are _____ by law.

   c. Peter was _____ for breaking the window.

   d. _____ someone else's children is a difficult thing to do.

   e. Littering is usually _____ by a fine.

3. **anxious**

   a. Chris is _____ to go home every summer vacation.

   b. A group of people were waiting _____ to receive their welfare checks.

   c. New students usually feel some _____ the first day of classes.

4. **restless**

   a. Her personal problems make her very _____ at night.

   b. Her doctor gave her some pills to overcome her _____.

   c. The patient was moving his body _____ as he waited for his turn to see the surgeon.

5. **displease**

   a. Charlie was afraid to _____ his supervisor by criticizing him.

   b. The sound coming from next door is very _____ to the ear.

   c. It is hard to face my parents' _____ when I do poorly in school.

6. **rise**

   a. Everyone had _____ even before the president entered the room.

   b. The sun _____ in the east.

   c. After several weeks of inability to walk, Mr. Brown finally _____ from his bed.

   d. The _____ sun is a symbol of hope.

7. **amaze**

   a. It is _____ that he could climb the World Trade Center.

   b. I was _____ at the tall buildings in New York when I first arrived.

   c. To our _____, she donated a large sum of money to the foundation.

   d. It still _____ me that my friend is a famous writer.

8. **tradition**

   a. It is a _____ in my family to get together on New Year's Day.

   b. _____, we would celebrate Christmas in December.

   c. Last Sunday, we enjoyed a performance of _____ dances from all over the world.

9. **rebel**

   a. At the age of sixteen, children start to _____ against their parents.

   b. He was excommunicated from his church because he was considered a

   _____.

   c. Many lives are often lost in a _____.

d. The psychiatrist was trying to understand the —————————— child.

10. tolerate

a. After living here for a few years, Mei-Lan was able to develop some

—————————— for foreign foods.

b. Sometimes my aunt finds her husband ——————————.

c. The police could no longer —————————— the students' unrest.

11. achieve

a. Finishing your college education is an ——————————.

b. Were you able to —————————— the goals set by your parents?

c. Doctors are —————————— some success in curing cancer patients.

12. engage

a. It is very difficult for me to —————————— in conversation with a stranger.

b. Larry and Rosie announced their —————————— date after the party.

c. I am —————————— in a project that deals with aging.

13. threat

a. Because of his insecurity, he considered everybody a ——————————.

b. The gangster —————————— him if he testified.

c. It is —————————— to discover that our food products are contaminated.

d. Pollution —————————— the health of city residents everyday.

14. antagonize

a. We do not understand why they feel —————————— toward each other.

b. Several actions have been taken to ease the racial —————————— that exists in the community.

c. My lawyer would never —————————— his clients even if they could not pay him.

15. forbid

a. Children are —————————— to see certain movies.

b. The Food and Drug Administration —————————— the use of certain drugs.

c. The old, ruined house had a —————————— look.

SYNONYMS

Rewrite each sentence choosing an appropriate synonym from the list below for each underlined word or phrase.

1. sternly	6. boldly	11. tolerate
2. bachelor	7. restless	12. raid
3. barbarous	8. blink	13. routine
4. nostalgic	9. antagonize	14. stammer
5. filial	10. traditional	15. scowl

1. My boss is an <u>unmarried man</u>.

_____

_____

2. After a fire, looters would <u>attack</u> the shops <u>suddenly</u>.

_____

_____

3. During the meeting, he <u>courageously</u> spoke up in favor of the senior citizens.

_____

_____

4. His wife gave him a <u>look of strong disapproval</u> when he started flirting with another woman.

_____

_____

5. He was dismissed from his job because of his <u>unrefined</u> behavior in treating his co-workers.

_____

_____

6. It has become a <u>usual procedure</u> for her to jog for one hour in the park before going to work.

_____

_____

7. It was difficult to fully understand what he was saying, because he <u>made involuntary pauses while speaking</u>.

8. The child waiting for his dentist was <u>constantly in motion</u>.

9. Her parents always treated her <u>strictly</u> whenever they had company.

10. Whenever Kim meets somebody from his hometown, he feels <u>homesick</u>.

11. The eye doctor requested the patient to <u>close and open his eyes</u> during the examination.

12. In many countries, marriage is celebrated in the most <u>conventional</u> way.

13. I do not <u>bear</u> pain very easily.

14. Pauline would have never <u>caused the hostility of</u> her best friend had she known the real truth of the matter.

15. Her attitude toward her parents was not conventionally <u>like a daughter's</u>.

Grammar

WORDS OF TRANSITION I

Transition is a word that comes to us from Latin and still has almost exactly the same meaning. *Trans* = across; *i* = go; *tion* = the act of. Put them all together, and *transition* means: "the act of going across." Applied to writing, it specifically means: "the movement from one idea to another, from one sentence to another, and from one paragraph to another."

Words of transition can be grouped into a number of different categories. We will consider three of these here.

1. *Time.* In the following paragraph, notice how the narrative moves smoothly through time by the use of the underlined words:

Wang San had no school <u>today</u>. But he hated Saturdays and Sundays because he had to eat all his meals at home. <u>Whenever</u> he saw the typical Hunan dishes, he lost his appetite. <u>Sometimes</u> he would sneak out and eat a hot dog or a hamburger before meals. If he had no money, he would raid the icebox <u>when</u> the cook wasn't in the kitchen. <u>When</u> he was very hungry, he would raid it anyway, cook or no cook. <u>Usually</u> he was hungriest when the family dinner was the richest, for there were so many delicacies on the table that Wang San hated. <u>Now</u> that he had learned his father was going to Westernize the household, he was excited.

2. *Space.* Time expressions are only one group of words that help a writer progress from one idea to another. Notice how this description uses words of transition to show space relationships:

We walked <u>across</u> the bridge, and <u>on the other side</u> we immediately saw the house we were looking for. It was only one story high with a small garden <u>in front of</u> it. Towering <u>above</u> it was a gigantic elm tree.

3. *Addition and Ordering of Ideas.* The paragraph below shows how writers can add one idea to another and indicate the importance of each by using the underlined words of transition:

There are several factors contributing to the high rate of inflation of the past year. <u>First</u>, the shortage of oil increased energy costs by 20 percent. <u>Moreover</u>, the coal industry strike led oil suppliers to raise prices even higher while the strike was in effect. <u>Second</u>, the severe frost in September ruined the wheat crop in many parts of the Midwest, contributing to higher food prices. <u>Equally important</u> in the food picture was the shortage of coffee. <u>Finally</u>, medical costs soared higher last year than they had in the previous five.

A. Read the first three paragraphs of the passage on page 71 and underline all the transition words relating to time.

B. Underline the transition words of both time and space in this paragraph.

Early in 1970 the college opened its new writing center in a small room behind the gymnasium. Later that year, the administration decided that the center was too far from the rest of the English department, so it was moved into a larger room near the other English offices. The following September, the writing center had so many clients that it was given an entire suite of rooms next to the library.

C. Using the following chart, fill in the blanks with appropriate words of transition. Try to use different words from each group.

Relationship Between Ideas	Words of Transition
Ordering according to time	next, then, now, immediately, soon, before, after, meanwhile, gradually, finally, suddenly, previously, subsequently, in the meantime, yesterday, today, tomorrow, just, already, at last, first, second, when
Ordering according to space	below, above, under, beyond, near, far, in front of, to the right, to the left, around, on one side, inside, outside, in back of, across
Ordering according to importance	more important, most important, equally important, first, second, third, next, last, finally
Addition	in addition, also, moreover, furthermore, too, again
Emphasis	in fact, indeed, certainly, again, undoubtedly, surely, truly, to repeat, actually

1. The results of the last experiment are very encouraging. (*emphasis*)

_____, they give us hope that we will soon find the cure for the disease that we have been studying so long.

2. There are several reasons why children should be encouraged to read books instead of looking at television. (*order of importance*) —————————————, they will learn concentration and self-discipline. ————————————, they will avoid the bad influence of excessive violence. ————————————, they will develop a skill that is essential to success in any career or profession.

3. It was so pleasant seeing you again after all these years. (*addition*)

   ———————————— it was fun to get news about my old friends.

4. Something caught his eye as he looked out of the window. (*space*)

   ———————————— there was a faint movement in the grass. (*time*)

   ———————————— he heard a strange noise.

5. Whatever you do, you must visit Paris. (*emphasis*) ————————————, some people consider it the center of the world. (*addition*) ———————————— you can travel easily to other parts of Europe from Paris.

6. She watched as the elevator door opened and about five people emerged. (*time*)

   ———————————— a young child on skates rolled out from the back of the elevator and bumped into her. ———————————— the elevator door had closed again and she was left waiting once more.

7. This course will cover grammar, spelling, and punctuation. (*addition*)

   ———————————— it will give you practice in writing. (*emphasis*)

   ———————————— it will require so much writing that you should learn to type to save time.

SENTENCE COMBINING

In combining these sentences, use a participial phrase or an infinitive phrase with a main clause instead of two clauses. You may find more than one possibility in some cases.

EXAMPLES

a. I looked through the pile of papers on my desk.
b. I finally found my lost assignment.

Looking through the pile of papers on my desk, I finally found my lost assignment. (*participial phrase*)

a. My teacher invited the entire class to her home.
b. She wanted to show her appreciation of our good work.

My teacher invited the entire class to her home to show her appreciation of our good work. (*infinitive phrase*)

1a. There were a lot of things.
  b. He had to do them at home.

_____

_____

2a. We saw Henry.
  b. He was shooting birds in the backyard.

_____

_____

3a. He could do all these things.
  b. He did not arouse his father's anger.

_____

_____

4a. Master Wang nodded his head.
  b. He wanted to show approval.

_____

_____

5a. He waited anxiously.
  b. He wanted his father to dismiss him.

_____

_____

6a. He was going down the hill.
  b. He saw Wang San throwing a leather ball.

_____

_____

7a. Master Wang felt anger.
  b. This anger was rising in him.

_____

_____

8a. Wang San hit the leather ball.
  b. Master Wang was amazed at that.

_____

_____

9a. Wang Ta tells me what to eat and what to wear.
 b. I do not like that.

_____

_____

10a. He went out of the house.
  b. He slammed the front door.

_____

_____

Writing Assignments

ESSAY TOPICS

Use at least three words from the vocabulary exercises. Remember to use words of transition where necessary.

1. Compare and contrast the teaching methods and classroom practices of your own country with those here. Show both similarities and differences. Your conclusion might indicate which you think are more effective.
2. Analyze your food preferences. Show which are related to your native country and which to your adopted one. Explain how some of your tastes changed or did not change.
3. Write a paper defining the generation gap in terms of its meaning for foreign students. Show how much of the gap is due to cultural conflicts between children and parents and how much is caused by problems that affect any modern family.
4. Discuss the cultural conflicts you have experienced since you came to this country. You may find it necessary to combine definition, comparison and contrast, and analysis in writing on this topic.

PROOFREADING

There are 11 errors in the following passage. Find and correct them. Note: Run-ons (comma splices) and sentence fragments each count as one error.

As a Haitian has studied in Haiti for many years and who is studying now in the United States, I find that the Haitian and American educational system are quite different from the other. What are their differences?

The first remark I make is that in American schools the student can choose among different options offered in one subject. This freedom does not exist in the Haitian curriculum. Although Haitian schools have different sections, such as A (Humanities), B (Languages), and C (Science). Only some famous private schools offer the C section. The Haitian is thus used to follow a rigid course distribution, and personnaly, I have been surprised by the freedom of choice given in the American system.

In Haiti, the student never has multiple-choices tests or true-or-false questions. He is also exposed to a very strict grading system where one almost never get 100, even if one deserves it. On the other hand, the passing grade is 50, thus my transcripts, if they have not been adjusted to American standards, might look very poor. When in reality they are not bad.

CHAPTER 7

The Threat of Deportation

When we first came, we worried every day that the authorities would find out we had entered illegally. But now we never think about deportation because everyone we know is in the same boat and no one has been caught yet.

From a Dominican student's paper.

READING PASSAGE

About the Author: When R. Mugo Gatheru was born, his tribe, the Kikuyus of Kenya, East Africa, expected him to become a *mundumugo* (similar to the American Indian "medicine man"), for his father, his grandfather, and their forefathers had been *mundumugos* for many generations.   However, after studying at the Medical Research Laboratory in Nairobi and working as an assistant editor for the Kenya African Union, he left Kenya to study at Lincoln University in Oxford, Pennsylvania, where he earned his B.A. under a full scholarship.   He continued his education and obtained an M.A. at New York University and a law degree from London University.   With his American wife, Gatheru returned to live in Kenya after it won independence from Britain.

To Think About: As you read, try to answer the following questions.   (See page xiii for reading guidelines.)

1. Why did Mugo go to India instead of coming directly to the United States?
   (Your answer will be the main idea of the paragraph.)
2. Judging from the agent's questions, what seemed to be his opinion of the Kenya African Union?
   (Your answer will be an implication.)
3. What were the events in Kenya that Mugo felt were connected with his interrogation?
   (Your answer will be the author's opinion.)
4. What was the problem caused by the second Immigration Office letter of Feb. 4, 1953?
   (Your answer will be the main idea of the paragraph.)

From
CHILD OF TWO WORLDS: A KIKUYU'S STORY

R. MUGO GATHERU

(Although not a member of the famous Mau Mau movement that fought for the independence of Kenya from Great Britain, Mugo Gatheru had written articles against racial discrimination before he left Kenya. At the time of the following incident, he was attending Lincoln University in Pennsylvania.)

On September 23, 1952, at about 11 A.M., the shadow of Mau Mau fell upon me. I had just finished my English class and was on my way to another class when a white man walked over to my professor and said: "Where is Mr. Gatheru?" The professor pointed me out to him. He walked over to me and showed me a card. It identified him as an agent of the United States Immigration Service. My heart sank. What did this agent want with me? He told me that he had been sent by the Immigration Service from Philadelphia to check on certain facts about my visa. He advised me to go and have my lunch first and to get excused from the rest of my classes for the day because the checking on these facts was going to take a long time. I didn't want any lunch. I said: "Let's start it right now."

I invited him to come to my room in one of the dormitories,* and I offered him a seat. He offered me a cigarette. Then he pulled some papers out of his bulky briefcase. I could not help noticing that he had a long list of questions in his hand. I started getting really frightened. My heart was beating furiously. I felt in the pit of my stomach* as if I had eaten a big meal that was weighing like a rock inside me. Did all of this mean that now, perhaps, I should never be able to get the higher education for which I had struggled so much?

The agent began to question me as though I were before a grand jury*:

---

dormitories Context clue: From the meaning of the sentence, it relates to rooms.

in the pit of my stomach Deep inside—an expression usually associated with a feeling of fear.

grand jury A special jury that determines whether there is enough evidence for a trial.

"What's your full name?"

"Reuel John Mugo Gatheru," I replied.

"How did you come to the United States?"

"I came to the United States by way of India and England," I answered.

"Why didn't you come to the United States directly from Kenya instead of going to India?" he asked.

"After I was offered a scholarship at Roosevelt College, I went to the American Consul in Nairobi to seek for information about the U.S. student visa. The American Consul advised me that in order to obtain a student visa, I had to get a certificate of good conduct or political clearance from the Kenya Government. I tried to obtain the necessary clearance, but all in vain. Hence, I went to India with a hope that if I did not obtain a U.S. visa, I could further my higher education in India."

"Who financed your trip to India?" he asked.

"My friends and relatives," I replied.

"You seem to have been very active in politics in Kenya. Can you tell me something about your activities in Nairobi?" he asked again.

"Well, first of all I went to Nairobi in 1945. I joined the Medical Research Laboratory as a learner laboratory technician. After some two years I left the Medical Department and joined the Kenya African Union as an assistant editor," I replied.

"What sort of literature were you editing?" he asked.

"A weekly newspaper published by the Kenya African Union," I replied.

"Any other literature?" he asked.

"Not to my knowledge," I replied.

"What was the Kenya African Union?" he asked.

"A country-wide political organization headed by Jomo Kenyatta whose main purposes were to secure African rights and self-government through constitutional means," I replied.

"Were you a member?" he asked.

"No, I was not a member officially, but there was nothing to prevent me becoming one."

"How could you be an assistant editor without being a member?" he asked.

"I was not compelled to join, as membership was quite voluntary. But do not think that because of this I did not fully support the union's policy."

"Was the Kenya African Union a communist body?" he asked.

"No it was not," I replied.

"Do you know of communists in Kenya?" he asked.

"No I don't," I replied.

"Is there a Communist Party in Kenya?" he went on.

"No, there is not," I replied.

"What's the population of Kenya?" he demanded.

"About 5,000,000 Africans, 100,000 Asians, and about 33,000 Europeans," I replied.

"Were you then an agitator for the Kenya African Union?" he insinuated.

"I was not an agitator* from the point of view of the Kenya Africans, but the Kenya settlers may have thought me one. After all, even George Washington was an agitator here in your country," I replied.

He laughed appreciatively but said nothing.

"Have you ever carried on any political agitation* in the United States, in India, in England?" he asked.

It was now clear to me that he thought that I had some kind of revolutionary aims.

"No," I answered.

I thought that even though my answers were genuine and clear, this man had a preconceived idea that I was a communist.

"What form of government would you like to see in Kenya?" he asked.

"A republican type of government," I replied.

"Who are your friends in the United States?" he asked.

"They are both white and black," I answered.

"Have you ever addressed or attended a meeting in the United States?" he asked.

"No," I answered.

"How do you support yourself financially?" he asked.

"I have a college scholarship," I answered.

"Are you supposed to perform some duties on completion of your college career, that is, after you have gone back to Kenya?" he asked.

At this I became angry. What kind of 'duties' could he mean? Why was he asking what I'd do when I went back home? Did all of this have something to do with the fact that there were disturbances in Kenya and, if so, what could he want from me?

"What are your major subjects here at Lincoln University?" he asked.

"History and political science," I replied.

"For what degree?" he asked.

"The B.A. degree," I replied.

Why this, I wondered? I still don't know, but it seemed obvious that the investigation had been initiated from overseas, that some kind of information must have been given to the immigration authorities by someone who knew me back in Nairobi.

The interrogation lasted from 11:15 A.M. until 2 P.M. The man was friendly in a detached, diplomatic way. I took his cigarettes and smoked them, but I was very angry at some of the questions. In fact, I was angry about the whole procedure. I asked him what was behind all this, and he said it was just a routine matter and that I should not worry. This was hardly the truth as we shall see later.

I reported the matter to Dr. Bond (President of Lincoln University).

---

agitator, agitation Context clue: "revolutionary aims" in the next paragraph.

He was disturbed and worried, but he said: "Just sit tight* and wait." He became very busy. He put everything else aside, including correspondence, and made several long calls to Philadelphia, New York, and Washington. He was thoroughly angry, particularly at those questions with which the immigration agent tried to implicate me with communism. At that time, American public opinion was very afraid of communism.

On October 20, 1952, only four weeks after my interrogation, the Kenya Government declared a state of emergency; two days later over a hundred leaders and officers of the Kenya African Union were imprisoned, including Jomo Kenyatta. I felt in my inner soul that these events must be connected with my interrogation although the immigration agent had said it only concerned my visa. Why were they concerned about my visa anyhow?

I never broke any immigration regulations, and each time I went to get my student visa renewed, I had no trouble at all. I never tried to hide anything from anybody. Once, I lost my passport and applied to Kenya for another one which they sent through the British Consulate General in Philadelphia. They knew exactly where I was. Everything I did was open and above board.* You can imagine my surprise when on November 5, 1952, six weeks after my interview with the immigration agent (and barely two weeks after the state of emergency had been declared in Kenya), I received a letter from the Immigration Office in Philadelphia which read as follows:

Dear Sir,

Pursuant to instructions received from the office of the Commissioner of Immigration and Naturalization at Washington, I request that you depart from the United States as soon as possible.

I am obliged to say that unless such departure is effected within thirty days, this office will be obliged to take the necessary steps to enforce your departure.

What did this mean? What had I done to warrant this expulsion?* Was it connected with the things happening in Kenya? Did the United States Government think that I had something to do with Mau Mau?

So, amid all my worries about the fate of my people at home, I now had my personal worries. I could hardly believe my eyes when I read the letter. I had struggled along until I had reached my junior year at Lincoln University. The fall term had just begun, and now the United States Immigration Office was telling me to get out. Where was I to go? To Kenya? I would certainly be thrown into a concentration camp immediately as a former assistant editor of the Kenya African Union newspaper. To Britain? What would I do there? I had no scholarship or means of support.

---

sit tight   Be patient and do nothing.

above board   Honest; not hidden.

expulsion   Context clues: base word is *expel*; its meaning is related to "enforce your departure" in the line above.

I wanted to stay in America to prepare myself to serve Kenya after the Mau Mau crisis was over. Now, I faced deportation. I had come to love Lincoln University and I wanted to get my B.A. degree from there.

I went in haste to Dr. Bond. He read the letter carefully, and I could see that he was getting more annoyed. He took the phone and made a call to Philadelphia. The immigration authorities refused to tell him why I was being ordered out of the country. He said he'd never take this lying down.* He started to work immediately to set up a committee to defend me.

It was rough. At night I could not sleep. I thought of numerous things as I was tossing around. Why am I suffering this much, I would ask myself? This was the price of my past activities in Kenya.

The students at Lincoln University were my real salvation. I was now a sort of hero, and they all came round and said: "Give them hell,* Mugo. We are with you." This gave me real strength, and I even began to enjoy the struggle.

People all over the United States rallied to my cause, and I fear that sometimes I really felt too important. Even the *New York Times* carried stories on me, and I began to hear that the Kenya papers were writing about the case too. The attempt by the immigration authorities to smear* me with communism did not stop people from supporting me. The American people were intelligent enough to understand that one did not have to be a communist to appreciate the fact that the Kenya settlers had more arable land than the Africans or that the living conditions in the Nairobi African locations were appalling! This was just everyday common sense.

My American friends fought so hard to save me from deportation that on February 4, 1953, I received a letter from the immigration authorities to say that:

> ... as a result of further consideration given to your status under immigration laws, you may ignore letter of this office dated November 5, 1952, requesting you to depart from the United States as soon as possible. In this connection, however, your attention is directed to the fact that your authorized stay in this country will expire on April 30, 1953, and you will be expected to depart by that date.

We had won a partial victory. I had been saved from deportation.

There was one fly in the ointment.* My visa was to run out two months before school closed. What was I to do?

---

take this lying down Accept without objecting.

give them hell Fight hard and hurt them.

smear Which dictionary meaning fits in this context?

fly in the ointment A problem in a situation that is otherwise positive.

(Mugo's lawyer, Jack Wasserman, decided to fight for a permanent visa so that Mugo could go on to graduate school and earn money while studying. He was forced to sue the U.S. government in a case which took four more years to settle.)

I am grateful to all my friends who made it possible for me to stay in America and to complete my studies there. I can't forget how scared I sometimes was and how sometimes I felt so much all alone. But I had faith in my lawyer and in my many friends. I knew that if we lost, it would not be because they hadn't tried as hard as they could to save me. This whole experience 'made a man out of me.' I do not regret it.

Comprehension

These questions are to be answered orally or in writing. Some of them may require more than one sentence for your answer.

1. What reason was given by the agent of the U.S. Immigration Service for questioning Mugo?
2. Why did Mugo refuse to eat lunch before he answered the questions of the Immigration agent?
3. Did the agent question Mugo in a formal or an informal manner? How do you know?
4. Why did Mugo go to India instead of coming directly to the United States?
5. What kind of work did Mugo do for the Kenya African Union?
6. Was the Kenya African Union a revolutionary organization? Explain your answer in terms of their purposes.
7. Did Mugo support the policies of the Kenya African Union?
8. Judging from the agent's questions, what seemed to be his opinion of the Kenya African Union?
9. What did Mugo mean by saying that George Washington was an agitator in America?
10. What did Mugo think was the reason for the investigation?
11. What was Dr. Bond particularly angry about?
12. What were the events in Kenya that Mugo felt were connected with his interrogation?
13. What did the Immigration Office letter of Nov. 5, 1952, order Mugo to do?
14. Why was Mugo afraid to return to Kenya?
15. What help did Mugo receive in his struggle against deportation?
16. What was the problem caused by the second Immigration Office letter of Feb. 4, 1953?
17. Why did Mugo sue the U.S. government for a permanent visa?
18. What is Mugo's attitude toward his experience?

DISCUSSION QUESTIONS

1. What kind of visa did you obtain to enter this country? What do you have to do to maintain your status? Have you had any problems with your papers since you came to this country? Did you feel that the immigration regulations were fair? If not, in what way should they be changed?

2. Were your family or friends active in politics in your own country? Have those activities had an effect on your life here? Do you participate in any political activities now? If so, what kind?

3. Has the form of government changed in your native country since you left? What was the change? How did it come about? Do you approve of the change?

4. Why did you leave your country? Do you intend to stay here or have you come only for an education? Do you intend to return? Is there any way in which you would like to help your countrymen?

5. Do you know of anyone who is in this country illegally? Why was he or she unable to enter legally? Do you believe that immigration should be limited or unrestricted? What difficulties does unrestricted immigration cause for the citizens of a country?

6. What are the immigration policies of your own country? Are they fair? How do they compare with the policies of the country in which you are now living?

CLOZE EXERCISE

Fill in each blank with a single (one) word.

On September. 23, 1952, at _____ 11 A.M., the shadow _____ Mau Mau fell upon _____. I had just finished _____ English class and was _____ my way to another _____ when a white man _____ over to my professor _____ said: "Where is Mr. Gatheru?" _____ professor pointed me out _____ him. He walked over to _____ and showed me a card. _____ identified him as an agent _____ the U.S. Immigration Service. _____ heart sank. What did this _____ want with me? He told _____ that he had been sent _____ the Immigration Service from Philadelphia _____ check on certain facts about _____ visa. He advised me to _____ and have my lunch first _____ to get excused from the _____ of my classes for the _____ because the checking on these _____ was going to take a _____ time. I didn't want _____ lunch. I said: "Let's start _____ right now."

I invited ——————— to come to my room ——————— one of the
dormitories, and ——————— offered him a seat. He ——————— me
a cigarette. Then he ——————— some papers out of ———————
bulky briefcase. I could ——————— help noticing that he had
——————— long list of questions in ——————— hand. I started getting really ———————.

Vocabulary

WORD FORMS

Fill in the blanks with the correct forms of the word given for each group of sentences. You may need the verb (changed where necessary for agreement or
tense), participles, a noun (singular or plural), an adjective, or an adverb. Sometimes the form may require negative prefixes such as *un-*, *dis-*, or *in-*.

1. **identify**

   a. The government is thinking of issuing ——————————— cards to all citizens.

   b. The witnesses to the crime were asked to ——————————— the murderer.

   c. The killer was ——————————— by one of the neighbors.

   d. His friends have difficulty in ——————————— his accent.

2. **organize**

   a. Mr. Fong was the one who ——————————— the International Club.

   b. Mary belongs to a nonprofit ——————————— which helps the community.

   c. Prof. Frazier's office looks so ———————————.

   d. The police department is trying to track down ——————————— crime in
      New York City.

3. **prevent**

   a. Medical schools are offering more courses in ——————————— medicine
      nowadays.

   b. Everybody was given a vaccine to ——————————— the spread of the
      disease.

   c. The fire department gave a workshop on fire ———————————.

   d. These pills will act as a ——————————— against malaria.

4. **settle**

   a. The Indians were the first ———————————————— in America.

   b. My friend is going to buy a house as soon as he is ————————————————.

   c. One can still see some early ———————————————— in the New England states.

   d. My cousin feels ———————————————— here because he has not found a job yet.

5. **revolt**

   a. Allowing students to engage in drugs on campuses is ————————————————.

   b. Many concerned citizens want to ———————————————— our society to make it a better world to live in.

   c. The guerillas in the Philippines ———————————————— against the government.

   d. He was not granted a visa to travel because he was considered a

   ————————————————.

   e. After the Cultural ————————————————, the Chinese became more self-reliant.

   f. The invention of the computer has ———————————————— the processing of information.

6. **enforce**

   a. Will the ———————————————— of capital punishment decrease crimes?

   b. John was assigned by the dean to ———————————————— the rules of the college.

   c. ———————————————— the laws against marijuana is almost impossible.

   d. The new immigration laws were ———————————————— to limit the entry of aliens.

7. **certify**

   a. You need a lawyer to ———————————————— that your papers are legal.

   b. She was presented a ———————————————— by the mayor for her heroic act.

   c. To be a public school teacher, one needs ———————————————— from the board of education.

8. **secure**

   a. Her well-paying job gives her a feeling of ————————————————.

   b. Elliot always lives with his mother because he feels ———————————————— living alone.

c. Robert _____ a permit to use the public library.

d. After she got her permanent visa to live in the country, she felt more confident and

_____.

9. **necessary**

a. What he said about Mary is not _____ true.

b. It is _____ for all aliens to report to the Immigration and Naturalization Department each year.

c. Water is a _____ in our daily life.

d. Her doctor was in favor of the operation, but the consultant believed it was

_____.

10. **authorize**

a. The chief engineer never _____ a highway project for the city.

b. Mary was given the _____ to hire a number of workers.

c. Her father is the only person _____ to sign for the family's properties.

d. The prosecutor needed _____ from the judge to dismiss the case.

11. **defend**

a. The lawyer tried to _____ his client in court.

b. He went to war because he believed in _____ his country.

c. Henry's firing two shots at the attacker was an act of _____.

d. The _____ presented excellent evidence for his argument.

12. **depart**

a. Her plane to Europe _____ from Kennedy Airport.

b. John was supposed to meet his friend in the _____ area.

c. We waved good-bye to our _____ friends.

d. His wife _____ suddenly for California without any warning.

13. **active**

a. Pressing this black button will _____ the missiles.

b. All citizens should be _____ in a political party.

c. The International Club offers many social _____ for foreign students.

d. Bob is _____ involved in his professional organizations.

14. **assist**

a. Residents and interns _____ physicians in the surgery room.

b. Mr. Brown was looking for a well-qualified _____.

c. The tutors give students _____ in their academic work.

d. Mr. Wu is _____ his professor in the math lab.

15. **worry**

a. Her father _____ too much about his children hanging out in the streets.

b. Peter's friend told him not to _____ if things didn't work out in the game.

c. John was very _____ when the police could not locate his missing son.

d. Stop _____ about not having enough money to buy new clothes.

SYNONYMS

Rewrite each sentence choosing an appropriate synonym from the list below for each underlined word or phrase.

1. deport	6. insinuated	11. implicate
2. agitator	7. warrant	12. initiated
3. smear	8. annoyed	13. procedure
4. emergency	9. genuine	14. correspondence
5. preconceived	10. visa	15. interrogation

1. The lawyer <u>suggested with suspicion</u> that the husband kept all the family wealth after the divorce.

_____

_____

2. The student gave the teacher a <u>sincere</u> answer to why he came late.

_____

_____

3. The government officials tried to <u>involve</u> the president with bribery.

_____

_____

4. The murderer was sentenced to death after <u>questioning</u> by the judge.

_____

_____

5. This organization was <u>originated</u> by a famous physician to help infants.

_____

_____

6. The country was in an <u>unexpected, serious situation</u> when martial law was established.

_____

_____

7. John forgot to apply for an <u>official authorization</u> to enter the USSR last year.

_____

_____

8. Juan Perez and Henry Lee did not understand what they had done to <u>justify</u> their leaving the country.

_____

_____

9. The Immigration Office has been trying to <u>expel</u> illegal aliens from this country.

_____

_____

10. Her competitors who tried to <u>stain</u> her with corruption did not succeed.

_____

_____

11. One can exchange <u>letters</u> with people from China without restrictions.

_____

_____

12. The committee agreed to a <u>course of action</u> to encourage students to major in liberal arts.

_____

_____

13. Her opinion of England was <u>already formed</u> before she even visited there.

_____

_____

14. The principal was very <u>irritated</u> when he found out that some students were taking drugs in school.

_____

_____

15. Anyone who voiced opposition was considered a <u>revolutionary</u> by the government.

_____

_____

Grammar

INFINITIVES USED WITH VERBS

Sometimes verbs are directly followed by an infinitive or an infinitive phrase (a group of words introduced by an infinitive).

EXAMPLES

I wanted <u>to stay</u>. (*infinitive*)

I wanted <u>to stay in America</u>. (*infinitive phrase*)

In the above sentences, the subject of the main verb, *I*, is also responsible for the action of the infinitive. However, in some sentences, a noun or pronoun coming between the verb and the infinitive is responsible for the action of the infinitive.

EXAMPLES

I invited <u>him</u> to come to my room.

They set up a <u>committee</u> to defend me.

Note that when a pronoun comes between a verb and an infinitive, as in the first example, it is in the object form (*him*).
An infinitive phrase can also follow an infinitive (or an infinitive phrase).

EXAMPLES

He promised <u>to try</u> <u>to obtain the money for my defense</u>.
                inf. + inf. phrase

I wanted <u>to stay in America</u> <u>to get my B.A. degree</u>.
          inf. phrase + inf. phrase

Furthermore, the subject of the main verb may not be responsible for the action of the second infinitive phrase.

EXAMPLE

This office will be obliged <u>to take</u> the necessary steps <u>to enforce your departure</u>.

In this case, the word "steps" governs the action of "to enforce your departure."
The sentence patterns described above are as follows:

1. Subject—Verb—Infinitive (Phrase)

   He   had been sent   to check on certain facts.

2. Subject—Verb—Noun or Pronoun—Infinitive (Phrase)

   He   advised   me   to have my lunch first.

3. Subject—Verb—Infinitive (Phrase)—Infinitive (Phrase)

   They   promised   to work hard   to assist me.

4. Subject—Verb—Inf. (Phrase)—Noun or Pronoun—Inf. (Phrase)

   They   did not forget   to send   the money   to pay for my lawyer.

GRAMMAR EXERCISES

A. Form sentences following pattern 2 above.

EXAMPLE

The veteran asked the president.
The president should help him.
The veteran asked the president to help him.

1. The speaker persuaded the crowd.
   The crowd should move away quietly.

   _____

   _____

2. His parents taught him.
   He should tell the truth.

   _____

   _____

3. The firm hired her.
   She should be sales manager.

   _____

   _____

4. The family expected me.
   I should arrive at 9 A.M.

   _____

   _____

5. His American friends encouraged Mugo.
   Mugo should continue his struggle.

   _____

   _____

B. Form sentences following pattern 3 above.

EXAMPLE

Their son is planning to go abroad.
He is going to study archeology.
Their son is planning to go abroad to study archeology.

1. No one had arranged to be at the airport.
   No one was there to meet his plane.

   _____

   _____

2. The witness failed to appear in court.
   The witness was to give testimony.

   _____

   _____

3. All students are required to report to the nurse.
   They must report to take an eye examination.

   _____

   _____

4. The nurse refused to leave the patient.
   She would not leave the patient to answer the telephone.

   _____

   _____

5. I hate to pretend.
   I would not pretend to agree with him because he is the boss.

   _____

   _____

   C. Form sentences following pattern 4 above.

   EXAMPLE
   She volunteered to notify the members.
   The members should come into the office for their assignments.
   She volunteered to notify the members to come into the office for their assignments.

1. I didn't want to remind him.
   He should take his medicine.

   _____

   _____

2. They are hoping to arrange a loan.
   The loan will pay for the new house.

   _____

   _____

3. Are you able to convince your friend?
   Your friend should contribute to our cause.

   _____

   _____

4. A few people started to incite the crowd.
   They incited the crowd to break store windows.

   _____

   _____

5. The government has agreed to ask industry.
   Industry must reduce its consumption of fuel.

   _____

   _____

SENTENCE COMBINING

Combine these sentences in the best way possible.   You may find more than one possibility in most cases.

1a. He told me.
  b. He had been sent by the Immigration Service.
  c. He had to check on certain facts about my visa.

   _____

   _____

2a. He advised me.
  b. I should have my lunch first.
  c. Checking on these facts was going to take a long time.

   _____

   _____

3a. First I was offered a scholarship at Roosevelt College.
  b. I then went to the American Consul in Nairobi.
  c. I went there to seek information about the United States.

   _____

   _____

4a. One of these papers was the _African Magazine._
  b. This magazine was published by some American Negroes.

c. These American Negroes lived in New York.

_____

_____

5a. I took his cigarettes.
 b. I smoked the cigarettes.
 c. However, I was very angry at some of the questions.

_____

_____

6a. I could never get a good conduct certificate.
 b. The certificate was from the Kenya Government.
 c. Therefore, the United States had never had a chance to refuse me.

_____

_____

7a. I lost my passport.
 b. I applied to Kenya for another one.
 c. This passport was sent through the British Consulate General in Philadelphia.

_____

_____

8a. I wanted to stay in America.
 b. I wanted to prepare myself to serve Kenya.
 c. I would serve when the Mau Mau crisis was over.

_____

_____

9a. Dr. Bond told me not to worry and to study.
 b. However, I was very worried.
 c. I could not keep my mind on my books.

_____

_____

10a. I am grateful to all my friends.
 b. My friends made something possible for me.
 c. I was able to stay in America.

_____

_____

WRITING ASSIGNMENTS

ESSAY TOPICS

Use at least three words from the vocabulary exercises. Remember to use words of transition where necessary.

1. Write an argument for or against unrestricted immigration into this country. (See page 67 for an outline of an argument essay.)
2. Write an essay about your work in a political, community, or school organization. This essay might involve both narration, including dialogue, and description.
3. Analyze the immigration policies of this country. What are the policies? Explain those which you consider good and those you think are bad. Come to a conclusion about the policies. (See page 44 for an outline of an analytical essay.) This topic will require some library research, but you can probably find the necessary information all in one article or book.
4. Compare the immigration policies of this country with those of your own country. Discuss such points as visas, other requirements for immigration, quotas and restrictions on immigration, and punishment for disobeying the regulations. (See page 20 for an outline of a comparison-contrast essay.)

PROOFREADING

There are 13 errors in the following passage. Find and correct them. Note: Run-ons (comma splices), misused infinitives, and sentence fragments each count as one error.

My friend would probably never of told me that he was here illegal, but one day I asked him to go with me to fill out some papers. I wanted him to intrepet for me if I did not understand the questions. He said he could not go. Because he was afraid someone would find out that he had no immigration papers. It was impossible for me hide my curiosity, so I asked him how had he come to this country. He said many people go to Puerto Rico, then they just fly to New York. Since Puerto Ricans are Americans, no one ask passengers from Puerto Rico for identification. My friend told me that he came first with his father, afterwards his mother came with his sisters. They were very poor in their own country and beleived life would be better here.   At first, they always afraid that the police will arrest them, but nobody asked any questions, not even their bosses.   Now they don't worry too much, but they avoid to go near an immigration office.

CHAPTER 8

Conflict of Loyalties

If my country wrongly invaded another country, I would accept condemnation of the action but not to the extent that it included our culture and institutions.   The criticism should only be for the leaders and not for the people.   Just because I belong to the country, why should they splash all the guilt on me?

From a Filipino student's paper.

READING PASSAGE

About the Author: Yoko Matsuoka left her native Japan to study in the United States at Swarthmore College, where she received her B.A. in 1939. She spent the years of World War II in Japan, returning to the United States in 1952 to study diplomacy and then traveling throughout most of the world. In Japan, she is known as both a writer and a social worker. As the author of books on North Vietnam, Madame Curie, and women's suffrage, Matsuoka is a member of P.E.N., the international writers' club. As a social worker, she has contributed much to women's social movements in Japan.

To Think About: As you read, try to answer the following questions. (See page xiii for reading guidelines.)

1. How was Yoko affected by the boycott of Japanese goods by the Swarthmore students?
   (Your answer will be the main idea of the paragraph.)
2. Yoko was *not* "convinced that Japan was all wrong." What were two of her arguments in support of her country?
   (Your answer will be supporting arguments.)
3. What was Yoko's opinion of the tea party for the Chinese and Japanese delegations?
   (Your answer will be the main idea of the paragraph.)
4. What did Yoko think should be done to stop wars?
   (Your answer will be the author's opinion.)

From
DAUGHTER OF THE PACIFIC

YOKO MATSUOKA

(*Yoko Matsuoka was a student at Swarthmore College in Philadelphia when Japan invaded Manchuria in 1936. The next year Japan seemed to be pushing into China, and many people condemned the Japanese.*)

A boycott of Japanese goods started in American colleges late that fall. My roommate had been born in China, and her missionary parents were still there. Naturally she had strong feelings for the Chinese people, and these she never bothered to conceal. Mano was among the first at Swarthmore to wear a "Boycott Japanese goods" pin.

One wintry day when we were walking to our room together, she proudly showed me her pin, the size of a fifty-cent piece. "Don't you think it's good, Yoko?" she insisted.

I made a sound in my throat which might have meant anything: "Hmmn . . ."

It was not that she was needling* me and I knew that. She was so proud of doing something which she felt right that she wanted to show off, and I appreciated her truthfulness. However, she did not realize that I, as the only Japanese on the campus, was taking the full burden of the situation upon myself, and it hurt.

Some persons, I think, participated in the boycott movement because they felt it would strengthen the liberal elements in Japan. I felt differently. I thought this would give the militarists all the more reason to insist that they had to protect Japan's interests where they could.

Twitter was another missionary child who boycotted Japan. Although attractive and intelligent, she did not appeal to many boys, so that a date was an event. One Saturday night she was getting dressed up in her one and only party dress to go out with a boy. Like other missionary children, she had very little spending money, and to her dismay she discovered that she did not have a pair of hose. She came to ask me whether I would lend her a pair. Intentionally I drew out my best pair of silk stockings, obviously a Japanese product, and presented them to her. She tenderly put

---

needling Context clue: The base word is *needle*. Literally, to needle someone would be to stick a needle into that person. What might it mean in the context of the passage?

them on her palm and seemed to ponder.* After a few minutes she returned them to me with a sigh and said, "Thanks just the same, Yoko." For that, I appreciated Twitter all the more.

(By 1938, the Japanese had taken most of the major Chinese cities.)

It was at the World Youth Congress, held at Vassar College in the summer of 1938, that I experienced emphatic* anti-Japanese sentiment. Drunk* with good intentions and self-righteousness,* hundreds of young people representing more than half the nations of the world condemned fascism, militarism and imperialism.

About thirty young Chinese were flown to the conference on the China Clipper. These representatives from "war-torn China" were hailed as though they alone were the symbol of resistance against the evils in the world. Among them was a young girl—rather homely and boyish with bobbed hair, wearing a simple blue Chinese cotton dress—who could not speak a word of English. Her qualification for attending the conference seemed to be that her parents had been killed by a Japanese bomb. When I heard this, I felt that I could not look her straight in the eye.

It pained me that a country of which I was a part was responsible for taking the lives of her parents and making her an orphan. Yet it seemed hypocritical for me to shake hands with her and say, "I apologize." I was sorry—perhaps more so than many others at the conference who shook hands with her and patted her on the shoulders. I knew it was against the rule of international law to kill civilians and that Japan was violating* the rules. But wasn't that modern warfare?

It was easy to say that Japan should be condemned because she was the aggressor. Legally, defensive war was permissible. But the right to decide whether or not a war was defensive was reserved for the nation at war. The Japanese Government, of course, insisted that she was merely defending her legitimate interests and that it was a threat to her national security to have an unfriendly neighbor such as China. Although I felt some other solution was more desirable, I could not be convinced that Japan was all wrong and others all right.

The fervor* and excitement of the conference did not sweep me away, but rather made me more sober* than before. I kept asking, "How can they be so sure that they are right?" I was disturbed and confused. And when a reporter from *Life* magazine interviewed me, I said with all sincerity: "I don't believe Japan knows how to bring about peace with the assurance shown by the delegates of other countries." When the magazine

---

ponder Context clue: the meaning of the sentence and the sentence following.

emphatic Context clue: adjective ending -*tic* for the base word *emphasis.*

drunk Is the word being used literally or metaphorically?

self-righteousness Context clues: the prefix *self*; base word is *right.*

violating Context clue: "against the rule."

fervor Context clue: "excitement."

sober Context clue: opposite of *excited.*

came out, I saw myself quoted as saying: "Japan does not know how to bring about peace. . . ." Although my letter of protest to the editor was published later, I heard that the Japanese police blacklisted* me for this remark.

This, however, did not discourage me from trying to get to know the Chinese students residing in International House in New York after the conference was over. I even made friends with a Korean girl who was notorious for her anti-Japanese sentiment. Some Japanese eyed me coolly for my conduct, but that only made me defiant. "This is the only place where I can come to know these people, and why shouldn't I?" I said. I was outraged when I heard that some Japanese called me unpatriotic. But I have somewhat enjoyed the uncomfortable role of being one of the minority ever since.

The World Christian Youth Conference, which met in Amsterdam that summer, was the first of its kind. Nearly a thousand young people, representing all denominations and many nationalities, assembled in this Dutch capital to discuss the problems of peace and the role of Christian youth in the world.

I joined the Japanese delegation of about a dozen young men and women, most of whom had come directly from Japan. They were extremely discreet* and their apparent reluctance to talk freely even among themselves indicated more than the usual Japanese reserve and politeness.

"How is the unemployment problem at home these days?" I asked one of the girls.

"There is no such problem."

"Really? What has happened to the several millions who were jobless in the early thirties? Have they just melted away?"

"I don't know, but we are not supposed to talk about unemployment," she answered uncomfortably.

Perhaps growing heavy industries had absorbed a great deal of man power. But it was this girl's attitude toward the problem which astonished me and gave me a glimpse of the pressure which I had to expect upon my return home.

The sponsors of the conference treated the Japanese delegation as though it were something fragile. I think they were sincerely glad that the Japanese could attend the conference, but they also seemed keenly aware that we represented the most "unchristian" nation in the world at that time. As there were no official delegates from Germany and Italy, the spotlight fell upon us as the aggressor.

China sent many delegates—many more than Japan. Somehow this war-torn country always managed to send large delegations to the various

---

blacklisted   Context clue: The *-ed* ending and position in the sentence show that the word *blacklist* is being used as a verb. If someone is blacklisted or put on a black list, what kind of list would it be?

discreet   Context clues: related to "reluctance to talk freely" and "reserve."

international conferences. I felt that the Japanese students should engage in a frank discussion with the Chinese and proposed this to our delegation. I believed that even if we did nothing else, we should talk with the Chinese. But others were reluctant. It was at a carefully planned tea party that the two groups finally met officially. Behind the steam rising out of our tea-cups, we put on our Sunday smiles* and exchanged friendly greetings. Sponsors were apparently relieved that there were no open clashes and embarrassment. Indeed it was a well-behaved party, but meaningless.

As I sat impatiently, exhibiting my best behavior, I recalled the World Youth Congress on the Vassar campus the year before. What a sharp contrast! It had been nerve-wracking then to be looked at with accusing eyes which said, "You alone are the enemy of humanity." But at the earlier meeting there was an electric* enthusiasm even though it failed to convince me as to the ultimate solution of the world problem.

Now in Amsterdam I was annoyed by the attitude: "You are wrong and I dislike you, but for the time being let's not talk about it." I asked myself: "Why can't we blow away this tea party steam between us and have a heart-to-heart talk? If Christians cannot talk frankly about the problems which separate them and come to a decision without killing each other, who can?"

I wonder now where that frank discussion that I so firmly advocated would have led us. Very likely nowhere. But it might have taught the young Japanese Christians to look at themselves with brutal truthfulness. It might have strengthened—instead of shaken—my faith in Christianity.

On the last day of the session a communion service was held, and for the first time all the denominations represented assembled together to share the common experience. "This is truly an ecumenical movement," many said with joy. It is ironical to look back to that day, remembering what followed only a month later. Christians of the world hailed the Amsterdam Conference because it succeeded in holding one mass communion when the most inhumane war mankind has experienced was just around the corner. Many have said apologetically since that a drop in the bucket* was better than none at all. But how inconsequential* that drop was! When it disappeared into the bucket, it immediately lost its identity.

(In the above paragraph, what happened a month after the communion service, in September, 1939, was the start of World War II, when Germany invaded Poland. Japan officially entered the war in December, 1941, when it attacked Pearl Harbor, but its war with China had been going on in the meantime. After Amsterdam, Yoko went to Geneva, Switzerland, the home of the League of Nations, from which Japan had withdrawn in 1933.)

Sunday smiles Yoko was a Christian, and therefore Sunday had a particular meaning for her. What would have been her idea of a Sunday smile?

electric Is this word being used literally?

a drop in the bucket An amount so small that it has no significance.

inconsequential Context clues: the prefix *in-*, meaning not or no; base word is *consequence*; *-ial* adjective ending.

There was not one Japanese in the beautiful international town when I arrived there. Even the Japanese Consulate had closed down.

The old gray and uninspiring Disarmament Building was being used as a lecture hall. In its basement I found an exhibition of war photographs sponsored by the Chinese Government. The purpose of the display seemed obvious: to show the cruelty of Japanese "aggression" in China. It was not easy to look at these pictures of bombed cities and suffering people, but I was determined to see every one of them. One photograph halted me, and it was to haunt me for many years afterward. It was a picture of a middle-aged Chinese woman dying on the street, apparently wounded by a Japanese bomb, and a child of about three, small and dirty, crying beside her. I could not take my eyes from the picture even after I had memorized every detail.

Bewildered and confused, I asked myself, "Was this necessary? Could we not have avoided it?"

Suddenly I saw a young Chinese approaching me. I remembered his face. He had been one of the delegates to the Amsterdam Conference. With a conquering smile and in a voice so loud that everyone around could hear, he said, "Now you know what the Japanese are doing to the Chinese."

I stared at him with dignity, I hoped, and did not say a word. What was there to tell him? Whatever I might have said would have been taken as either a bad excuse or a timid apology, and what I had in my mind was neither. It would have been something like this: "Yes, it was unbearably brutal, but modern warfare is that. Moreover, the distinction between civilians and combatants no longer exists as it once did. I realize this does not excuse war itself. But it is the causes of war which we must study and cure."

I was back at the same place where I found myself after the World Youth Congress. I was still not convinced that Japan was entirely to blame for the disorder and chaos* in the world.

I was staying in a small pension* during my week in Geneva. There I was among students from the United States, Canada, England, Germany and Norway, most of whom were attending the Institute of Higher International Studies. Dinner time was gay and enjoyable, for we all ate together at a big round table.

The boys used to say half jokingly: "The next meeting place will probably be on a battlefield."

It was indeed too gloomy a prospect, and yet they said it again and again and laughed. "Why must they mention it?" I wondered. They almost seemed to find pleasure in these words, and I could not understand. Perhaps they sensed that war could not be avoided, that it was coming

---

chaos Context clue: "disorder."

pension Context clue: From the sentence, "I was staying in a small pension . . . ," it is clear that the usual meaning of *pension* does not apply.

within a frightfully short time, and there was nothing they could do to prevent it. Hating to admit that they were merely pawns* in the world of power politics, they had come to Geneva to study in the hope of finding a solution. The flip remark was an expression of foreboding born of a wish to conceal their fears.

I have lost the names and addresses of these young men, although I can still see some of their faces. I wonder who else is alive to remember those delightful evenings at a Swiss pension only a little more than ten years ago?

---

pawns   Is this being used literally?

Comprehension

These questions are to be answered orally or in writing. Some of them may require more than one sentence for your answer.

1. How was Yoko affected by the boycott of Japanese goods by the Swarthmore students?
2. Did Yoko support the boycott? What was her reason for her opinion?
3. Why did Yoko particularly appreciate her friend Twitter?
4. In what way were the Japanese condemned at the World Youth Conference of 1938?
5. What was Yoko's reaction to the young Chinese girl whose parents had been killed by a Japanese bomb?
6. Yoko was *not* "convinced that Japan was all wrong." What were two of her arguments in support of her country?
7. Why did the Japanese police blacklist Yoko?
8. What else did Yoko do that some Japanese did not approve of?
9. At the conference in Amsterdam, why was the Japanese delegation reluctant to talk about unemployment in Japan?
10. What was Yoko's opinion of the tea party for the Chinese and Japanese delegations?
11. What was the reason for her opinion?
12. What kind of discussion would Yoko have preferred?
13. In Yoko's opinion, what was the value of the mass communion service held on the last day of the Amsterdam conference?
14. What was the reason for her opinion?
15. How did Yoko feel about the war photographs she saw on exhibit in Geneva?
16. Did Yoko apologize for what the Japanese had done to the Chinese?
17. What was Yoko's opinion of the killing of Chinese civilians?
18. What did Yoko think should be done to stop wars?
19. Why did the young men at Geneva laugh about the idea of fighting on a battlefield?

DISCUSSION QUESTIONS

1. Have you ever participated in a boycott of goods or food? If so, what was the purpose of the boycott? Do you think boycotts are effective?
2. In 1939, Yoko Matsuoka believed that in a modern war the killing of civilians could not be avoided. Do you agree with her opinion? Since 1939, has the situation changed at all? Have more or fewer civilians been killed in wars since that time? Discuss specific wars.

3. In 1939, Germany, Japan, and Italy were considered fascists, militarists, and imperialists. Discuss the meaning of these words. Are these three countries still called by these names? In recent years, have these labels been applied to different countries? Which ones? Why?

4. Do you agree with the policies and actions of your own country? Have you ever had to defend them against the opinion of people who criticized them? Which do you think is more important—loyalty to one's country or justice? Why? If your country became involved in a war, would you help it?

5. Yoko thought that it was ironical to remember the mass communion service which took place only one month before the start of World War II. What does *ironical* mean? How does the word apply to the situation described by Yoko?

CLOZE EXERCISE

Fill in each blank with a single (one) word.

About thirty young Chinese were flown _____ the conference on the China Clipper. _____ representatives from "war-torn China" were hailed _____ though they alone were the symbol _____ resistance against the evils in the _____. Among them was a young girl— _____ homely and boyish with bobbed hair, _____ a simple blue Chinese cotton dress— _____ could not speak a word of _____. Her qualification for attending the conference _____ to be that her parents had _____ killed by a Japanese bomb. When _____ heard this, I felt that I _____ not look her straight in the _____.

It pained me that a country _____ which I was a part was _____ for taking the lives of her _____ and making her an orphan. Yet _____ seemed hypocritical for me to shake _____ with her and say, "I apologize." _____ was sorry— perhaps more so than _____ others at the conference who shook _____ with her and patted her on _____ shoulders. I knew it was against _____ rule of international law to kill _____ and that Japan was violating the _____. But wasn't that modern warfare?

Vocabulary

WORD FORMS

Fill in the blanks with the correct forms of the word given for each group of sentences. You may need the verb (changed where necessary for agreement or tense), participles, a noun (singular or plural), an adjective, or an adverb. Sometimes the form may require negative prefixes such as *un-*, *dis-*, or *in-*.

1. **bother**

   a. When Pierre is studying in his room, he does not want anybody to

      _____ him.

   b. Stop _____ me or else I'll report you to the police officer.

   c. Taking three trains to come to school is a big _____.

2. **participate**

   a. The actors _____ in the scene were stopped by the director.

   b. Not every employee _____ in the company stock plan.

   c. Good teachers usually encourage students' _____ in class.

   d. He did not _____ in the Olympic Games because he had an accident.

3. **discover**

   a. While working on her experiment, Charlotte made a new _____.

   b. The child _____ that his mother hid the cookies in the cabinet.

   c. Do you know who the _____ of mercury is?

4. **produce**

   a. Some countries in Asia export their entire _____ of coconut.

   b. What is the quality of the _____ you get in the supermarket?

   c. Big companies retain workers whose _____ is high.

   d. The college theater department _____ a play last week.

5. **condemn**

   a. One should not _____ a person before a thorough investigation of the case.

   b. A person _____ by the press has no hope for a fair trial.

   c. The critic's _____ of the book did not prevent it from becoming a best-seller.

6. **resist**

    a. He could not _____ the temptation of eating the dessert.

    b. During the winter season, many people get sick because their

        _____ is low.

    c. Why are you _____ the wonderful job offer?

    d. The draft _____ were given amnesty.

7. **qualify**

    a. After the interview, he was told that he was not _____ to teach
        on the college level.

    b. Dennis has all the _____ to get into Harvard Law School.

    c. Do you _____ to play in the tennis tournament?

    d. She passed the test _____ her as an accountant.

8. **responsible**

    a. Each student should be _____ for the work assigned in class.

    b. The doctor has the _____ of letting patients know their condi-
        tion before surgery.

    c. John was dismissed from his job because he was _____.

9. **apology**

    a. One has to learn when to _____ after making a mistake.

    b. He owes you an _____ for talking to you rudely.

    c. He always acts _____ even though everything goes right.

10. **violate**

    a. Do not _____ traffic laws.

    b. Two businessmen were imprisoned for _____ of the obscenity
        regulations.

    c. Do you think illegal aliens are _____ the immigration laws?

11. **aggressive**

    a. Is an _____ personality an asset or a liability?

    b. Business people must act _____ to become successful.

    c. The _____ of the big powers was discussed in the conference.

    d. In many wars, each party claims the other was the _____.

12. **legitimate**

    a. The committee came up with a _____ solution to the problem.

    b. Society is more accepting of _____ children than it was a century ago.

    c. The prosecutor acted _____ in demanding severe punishment for the crime.

13. **outrage**

    a. The massacre was an _____ to the civilized world.

    b. Incompetence _____ Peter.

    c. I thought it was _____ that he spent so much money on clothes.

14. **discuss**

    a. Mature people _____ a problem to avoid misunderstanding.

    b. He carried on the _____ for almost two hours.

    c. He invited several _____ to the conference.

15. **shake**

    a. You must _____ the bottle first before opening.

    b. I _____ severely _____ up in the car accident.

    c. I saw his legs _____ when he stood up to give his speech.

    d. He ordered a milk _____.

    e. She received a salt _____ for a birthday gift.

    f. A severe earthquake _____ the ground last night.

SYNONYMS

Rewrite each sentence choosing an appropriate synonym from the list below for each underlined word or phrase.

1. frank	6. boycott	11. civilians
2. dismay	7. ecumenical	12. denominations
3. conceal	8. appeal	13. threat
4. fragile	9. discreet	14. security
5. sentiment	10. hypocritical	15. notorious

1. Mary never bothers to <u>hide</u> her feelings toward the women's liberation movement.

_____

_____

2. A group of demonstrators was standing in front of the supermarket trying to persuade people <u>not to buy</u> grapes.

_____

_____

3. Jane's younger sister <u>attracts</u> many of her friends because of her liveliness and intelligence.

_____

_____

4. To her <u>discouragement</u>, she failed the course in history.

_____

_____

5. Kathy felt it was <u>insincere</u> for her to tell Charles that everyone in the class liked him.

_____

_____

6. During World War II, many <u>nonmilitary people</u> were imprisoned and killed.

_____

_____

7. Eating too much sugar is a <u>possible danger</u> to one's health.

_____

_____

8. Some Chinese found <u>safety</u> in Hong Kong after escaping from China.

_____

_____

9. A supervisor has to be very <u>tactful</u> when dealing with his or her workers.

_____

_____

10. There is a <u>universal</u> movement to unite all Christian churches.

_____

_____

11. Their relationship was strengthened after an <u>honest</u> discussion of the problem.

_____

_____

2. The package that she mailed was marked "<u>delicate</u>, breakable."

_____

_____

13. Robert expressed his <u>feelings</u> for the foreign students in his speech at the club.

_____

_____

14. He is <u>well known</u> for his unpleasant criticism of other people's work.

_____

_____

15. All the <u>religious groups</u> were invited to provide extracurricular activities for community people.

_____

_____

Grammar

PARTICIPIAL MODIFIERS

As discussed in chapters 2 and 3, the present participle occurs in phrases which act as modifiers of nouns and pronouns.

EXAMPLES

It was pleasant to see the entire class <u>participating in the performance</u>.

<u>Moving through the crowd</u>, she met several people she knew.

Present participles are also used as one-word adjectives.

EXAMPLE

It was not easy to look at these pictures of <u>suffering</u> people.

Similarly, the past participle may also serve as an adjective or introduce a modifying phrase.

EXAMPLES

The pictures showed many <u>bombed</u> cities.

It was at the World Youth Congress, <u>held at Vassar College in the summer of 1938</u>, that I experienced emphatic anti-Japanese sentiment.

The past participle as a modifier is clearly related to its use in passive verb forms.   (See ''The Passive Form of Verbs'' in chapter 1.)

EXAMPLE

The pictures showed many cities that <u>had been bombed</u>.   (*passive verb*)

The pictures showed many <u>bombed</u> cities.   (*past participle*)

On the other hand, the present participle is used if it relates to an active verb.

EXAMPLE

It was pleasant to see the entire class as it <u>participated</u> in the performance. (*active verb*)

It was pleasant to see the entire class <u>participating</u> in the performance. (*present participle*)

These active and passive relationships can help in deciding which form of the participle to use as a modifier.

EXAMPLES

Active verb: The story <u>pleased</u> the children.

Present participle: It was a <u>pleasing</u> story.

Passive verb: The children <u>were pleased</u> by the story.

Past participle: They were <u>pleased</u> children.

GRAMMAR EXERCISES

A. Fill in the blanks with the correct participle.

1. The incident disturbed many people.

   It was a _____ incident.

2. Many people were disturbed by the incident.

   There were many _____ people.

3. Her reaction to my book encouraged me.

   It was an _____ reaction.

4. The clothing has been ironed very neatly.

   It is neatly _____ clothing.

5. The Greek meal satisfied the diners.

   It was a _____ meal.

6. The diners were satisfied by the meal.

   They were _____ diners.

7. His attitude disgusted me.

   He had a _____ attitude.

8. Our clothing was torn by the washing machine.

   We had _____ clothing.

9. Charcoal purifies water.

   Charcoal is a _____ substance.

10. The play disappointed the audience.

    It was a _____ play.

11. Words which are spoken are more powerful than those which are written.

    _____ words are more powerful than

    _____ ones.

12. The book bored the critics.

    It was a _____ book.

13. The dog barked all night long.

    It was a _____ dog.

14. The wind blew the leaves.

    They were _____ leaves.

15. The birds flew south in the winter.

    They were _____ birds.

B. Rewrite the following sentences replacing one of the clauses with a participial modifier (either one word or a phrase, as appropriate).

EXAMPLES

Hundreds of young people who represented more than half of the nations of the word condemned fascism.

Hundreds of young people <u>representing</u> more than half of the nations of the world condemned fascism.

These representatives were from China, which was torn by war.

These representatives were from war-<u>torn</u> China.

1. Among them was a young girl who wore a simple blue Chinese cotton dress.

_____

_____

2. I tried to get to know the Chinese students who resided in International House.

_____

_____

3. The two groups met officially at a tea party that was carefully planned.

_____

_____

4. As I sat impatiently and exhibited my best behavior, I recalled the Youth Congress of the year before.

_____

_____

5. I found an exhibition of war photographs which was sponsored by the Chinese government.

_____

_____

6. It was a picture of a middle-aged woman who had apparently been wounded by a Japanese bomb.

_____

_____

7. There was a child of about three, small and dirty, who was crying beside her.

_____

_____

8. Suddenly I saw a young Chinese who was approaching me.

_____

_____

9. They hated to admit that they were merely political pawns, and they tried to find a solution.

_____

_____

10. The flip remark was an expression of foreboding which was born of a wish to conceal their fears.

_____

_____

SENTENCE COMBINING

Combine these sentences in the best way possible. You may find more than one possibility in most cases.

1a. We were walking to our room together.
 b. She proudly showed me her pin.
 c. The pin was the size of a fifty-cent piece.

_____

_____

2a. She was attractive.
 b. She was intelligent.
 c. However, she did not appeal to many boys.

_____

_____

3a. There was a young girl.
 b. This girl was wearing a simple blue Chinese cotton dress.
 c. She could not speak a word of English.

_____

_____

4a. It was easy to say.
 b. Japan should be condemned.
 c. She was the aggressor.

_____

_____

5a. This did not discourage me from trying.
 b. I was trying to get to know the Chinese students.
 c. These Chinese students were residing in International House in New York.

_____

_____

6a. I made friends with a girl.
 b. The girl was Korean.
 c. She was notorious for her anti-Japanese sentiment.

_____

_____

7a. The conference was the first of its kind.
 b. The conference was a World Christian Youth Conference.
 c. The conference met in Amsterdam that summer.

_____

_____

8a. Nearly a thousand young people assembled in the Dutch capital.
 b. These young people represented all denominations and many nationalities.
 c. Their purpose was to discuss the role of Christian youth in the world.

_____

_____

9a. I sat impatiently.
 b. I exhibited my best behavior.
 c. I recalled the World Youth Congress on the Vassar campus the year before.

10a. On the last day of the session, a communion service was held.
  b. For the first time all the denominations represented assembled together.
  c. The purpose of this assembly was to share the common experience.

Writing Assignments

ESSAY TOPICS

Use at least three words from the vocabulary exercises. Remember to use words of transition where necessary.

1. Write an essay about a conference that you attended or a boycott or demonstration in which you participated. You might use both description and narration for the event itself and analysis to show whether the desired aim was achieved.
2. Should nations at war be condemned for the killing of civilians? Are there circumstances when the killing of civilians is acceptable? Take a position on this issue and write your arguments in support of your opinion.
3. Write an analysis of Yoko Matsuoka's comments on the actions of the Japanese against the Chinese in the years 1937–1939. Was she objective or subjective in her views? Was she logical? Be sure to come to a conclusion about her attitude.
4. Write a paper on the topic of loyalty to one's country versus one's conscience (what one believes is right). Which do you believe is more important? This would involve definitions of loyalty and of what is morally right, as well as argumentation.

PROOFREADING

There are 13 errors in the following passage. Find and correct them. Note: Run-ons (comma splices) each count as one error.

I will not commit the fallacy of attacking the author, yet many paragraphs of that passage revealed inconsistencies. It was an unfortunate event for her be caught in the world of power politics. She must had realized that she had nothing to do with her country's aggresion, but because of her loyalty, she presented contradictions for herself instead of uphold her integrity. She explained that even Japan was the aggressor, she was merely defending her legetimate interests. I thought it was really naive for her to utter those statement. At least, she didn't make any apology for Japanese brutality, otherwise she would have seemed hypocritical. Still, "modern warfare" is no excuse for brutality. Most people can sense what is brutal act. I doubt very much that brutality can be wipe away so casually.

When I was in Japan, I visited the War Museum of Nagasaki. It is a four-story building near the atom-bomb site. Inside it pictures and remains are exhibited which are a thousand times more horrible than what the author had seen in Geneva. I personally felt those kind of destruction was awful, and naturally I wondered why the American Arm Forces used a cannon to shoot a mouse.

CHAPTER 9

Interracial Marriage and Discrimination

There was a hue and cry among my family and friends when I told them I was marrying an African girl. Since I let them know the news, I have faced many incidents because of their disagreement with my decision. I think an interracial marriage needs a lot of guts and love to succeed.

From an Italian student's paper.

READING PASSAGE

About the Author: Raymond Joseph has called himself a "Christian revolutionary" in describing his activities opposing the former dictator of Haiti, François Duvalier, known as "Papa Doc." When Joseph returned to Haiti after obtaining a college degree in the United States, he helped many students and others who were hiding from Duvalier's secret police. Forced to leave Haiti because of the danger to his life, Joseph continued his anti-Duvalier activities in the United States and was condemned to death *in absentia* by Duvalier.

To Think About: As you read, try to answer the following questions. (See page xiii for reading guidelines.)

1. In describing the political and social structure of Haiti and his own position within it, the author presents his conclusions about the various situations in which he finds himself and his family. What are these different conclusions?
   (Your answers will be the author's opinions and conclusions.)

2. Mr. Joseph comes from Haiti, where, we are told, the peasant classes speak Creole. Is this the only language that he understands? How do you know? When Mr. Joseph emigrates to the United States, what new languages does he master? Why is the study of language so important to him?
   (Your answers will be supporting details.)

3. Explain how Moody Bible Institute is hypocritical about its rule on interracial dating.
   (Your answer will be supporting details.)

4. What is the author's response to the idea that interracial marriages can't work?
   (Your answer will be the author's opinion.)

INTERRACIAL MARRIAGE
AND DISCRIMINATION

RAYMOND A. JOSEPH

I was brought up in a Christian home. My father is a Baptist minister who thought—perhaps still does—that the call of God* to the ministry, at home or abroad, is the highest one. My father is now serving in the mission field in Guadeloupe. In 1969 at sixty-seven, my mother died there—an exile.

When my parents left Haiti in 1965, they never expected their visit to the United States, "for rest," would take them to the mission field. They knew very little of my revolutionary activities, although they were aware of my vehement opposition to the tyranny in my country. Since I was becoming more and more outspoken against the Haitian tyrant, many feared for the safety of my parents. My father finally agreed that I was doing the right thing. "A voice must be raised against injustice and terror," he said. As my parents' "vacation" was prolonged, my father was replaced as president of the Association of Evangelical Baptist Churches of South Haiti.

As a young Christian I became concerned about the duality of Haitian culture. The "elite" of the nation (less than 5 percent of the population) thought of Haiti as another French country. To speak French, to behave like "colonials" among the poor, was the greatest attainment of the ruling class. No more than 20 percent of the people spoke, read or understood French. Eighty percent of the Haitians knew only Creole, a language derived mainly from French and West African languages with English, Spanish and Carib Indian words thrown in. All Haitians, even the educated, felt more at ease in Creole. At fifteen I was teaching peasants to read and write Creole. At nineteen I began the first Christian print shop in South Haiti for the West Indies Mission, an American faith mission. We put out the first Creole-language paper. It still exists.

I graduated from the mission's Bible school and became assistant pastor of the main church of the Haitian Association. Later I spent one year in a little church back in the mountains where I gained much experience among Haiti's real people, the peasants who represent 85 percent of the population. I taught myself English and became a translator and interpreter at the mission compound. Making Philippians 4:13* ("I can do all

By permission of the author, Raymond A. Joseph.

---

the call of God The idea that one has been destined by God to serve in the church.

Philippians 4:13 The eleventh book of the *New Testament*.

things in him who strengthens me") my life verse, I decided that I would go to the United States to study biblical languages, to put the Bible into Creole. My father upbraided me for my "wild dream," pointing out that he was not a rich man.

The missionaries were not enthusiastic about the project. Some said that I would be dazzled by the "bright lights" of the city. This was the reason advanced by Prairie Bible Institute missionaries who felt that if I must go abroad, the campus in Alberta, Canada, would be ideal. Others spoke of the social problems which I, a black, would encounter.

When I was finally leaving for the Moody Bible Institute in Chicago, the director of our mission said: "I fear that you may not get the same welcome in the States that we get here. You may turn very antimissionary." He meant that while white missionaries were well received in Haiti, a black convert coming to the places which sent the missionaries would find unpleasantness.

An American black Baptist minister from North Carolina visited Haiti in April, 1954. He wanted a native interpreter. I was the only one available. He offered to help me if ever I decided to study in America. I told him about my project, whereupon he said to count on him. A poor man of God himself, he was rich in friends and faith. By August he had raised enough funds to pay for my one year at the Moody Bible Institute. (There would be no need for more, since the school had accepted me "by faith" for only a year. I had no high school diploma, which meant I would not graduate.) I came to Moody. I enrolled in the pastor's course and graduated, with honors, in 1957—having passed an entrance test at the University of Illinois to meet the high school requirements. My Baptist minister friend remained faithful throughout. He and his family even "adopted" me as their Haitian son and brother.

The pastor's course at Moody was the only one at that time which offered Greek and Hebrew, languages I needed for Bible translation. I began translation work in March, 1957, under the auspices of the American Bible Society and worked at it for six years. Others before me had labored on the translation, but the task of finishing the job and coordinating the whole fell on my shoulders. The New Testament with Psalms in the Creole of Haiti was on the market by June, 1960. I was a happy man. I continued to translate selected books of the Old Testament and assisted with a popular French version.

I also entered Wheaton College in 1957 but graduated *in absentia*. I had caused an uproar in 1959 by marrying a white American girl whom I met at Moody. Beth was a music major who loved French. Her voice was a big asset for the Moody Chorale. I coached her in French. Moody forbade interracial dating, a ruling kept on file at the deans' offices but which for some unexplained reason did not appear in the Moody Student Handbook. The ruling covered all possible interracial combinations—Asiatic-Caucasian, Caucasian-Negro, Negro-Asiatic.

Beth and I fell in love. Our romance blossomed at the senior retreat, chaperoned by the deans, at a vacation ranch in Michigan in the fall of

1956. We saw each other often that last year in school. It was an open secret* for many students, but apparently no one told the deans. I should say that besides my girl, that year I had won the "most popular male senior award" by the secret ballots of the students.

Beth stayed at Moody for postgraduate work while I went on to Wheaton—she wanted to accompany the Moody Chorale in their tour of Europe in the summer of 1958 and also worked for the Salvation Army. I was happy that now I could take my girl to all school activities, for I thought Wheaton more liberal than Moody. The dean soon called me in to say that my "comportment" was "offensive" to some people. He admitted that the people he referred to were the administration and some of the faculty. At this time I lived with a white American family that included three young children. They all liked me and accepted Beth. The International Students (a campus club) had voted me their president, and I was an officer of the Anthropology Club. But I could not bring Beth to the "Artists Series" on campus.

I will never forget the pained look on the face of the Wheaton dean when I asked him if I could take Beth to a concert at Orchestra Hall in Chicago. He said: "Yes, you may do whatever you want, but don't bring her on campus."

"You mean I can take my girl to all those worldly places but I cannot come with her to the holy place of God?"

The stage had been set for refusing me permission to marry. All Wheaton students—freshmen are ineligible—must request permission a month in advance before getting married. I had made my request three months in advance. The dean called me to his office to announce that the committee had turned me down. My fiancee's parents opposed the marriage, the dean explained. Did Wheaton consult *my* parents? No. By this time my fiancee had left Moody and had been supporting herself for three years. But the Wheaton and Moody deans had cooperated to contact my fiancee's parents.

When the dean refused to give me permission, I asked what would happen if I married without permission and he said: "You will be expelled." So I married without permission. The dean called me in and asked that I sign a withdrawal card. I refused, stating that I did not find it necessary to withdraw. I was ready to sign if the form had been an expulsion card and had read, "Wheaton College finds it necessary to expel Mr. Joseph."

The dean said I could not go to class. I accepted the verdict, but not without adding, "I will not give you the satisfaction of kicking myself out. You will have to do that."

The campus was in ferment. Petitions in my favor were circulating among the students and signatures were being collected. The Interna-

---

open secret: How much of a secret is an "open" one?

tional Students were organizing to march on President Edman's house to request justice for a fellow international. The student newspaper, *Wheaton Record,* published a caustic commentary on April 30, 1959, about "an idealistic young man" who "once came to 'the Land of the Free and the Home of the Brave' seeking an education, friends and perhaps the answer to a riddle . . . a riddle about color. . . . He received at least part of his education. He even made a number of friends. But the answer to his riddle came in an unsuspected manner. . . . The answer was that color does separate. . . . This is the real tragedy, for nothing is able to wound as deeply as hypocrisy."

The controversy raged for a week. A fellow international student became a conciliator. He said that the dean wanted to see me. I went to the office. The dean said, "You cannot go to class."

I said: "I will not sign your withdrawal card. Neither will I go to the newspapers [the school feared publicity], for by the time the story gets back to my country and to Latin America, it may be twisted to say that a Negro was lynched at Wheaton College because he married a white girl. That will not help you with your motto 'For Christ and His Kingdom.'"

The dean said, "You have acted in a more Christian manner than we."

An agreement was worked out. My wife would supervise me as I wrote my final examinations at home. A full year later, I wrote my finals after I had received three notices from Wheaton saying that my degree was waiting. I won honors on my examinations, and my B.A. in social anthropology was mailed to me.

The Wheaton College incident reminded me of what had happened to me and a fellow black American when we visited in Jackson, Mississippi, in the summer of 1955. We were ushered out of a Saturday-night Youth for Christ rally at the Hotel Edwards, although the YFC secretary had told me on the telephone, "Brother Joseph, you will be most welcome." I had explained that I was from Haiti, a student at Moody, and that I usually attended YFC meetings in Chicago. When the embarrassed secretary led us to the elevator, I told him, "Thank you for your Christian welcome." To an elderly lady who was protesting the action against "this visitor from Haiti," I said, "Don't worry. If this isn't youth for Christ, I do not want to stay."

Over the next twelve years, my wife and I had four children, while I became increasingly active in Haitian political organizations in the United States. For many reasons, to be described later, our marriage—like the marriages of so many other Americans—gradually broke down. I got a legal separation in 1971 and was divorced in 1973. Certainly those who, years earlier, opposed the marriage may have reassured themselves with "I told you so; interracial marriages can't work." This simplistic reasoning fails to take into account what is happening in the society at large.

Something which is readily observable has been confirmed by the U.S. Census Bureau: The tempo of divorces has quickened. In 1970 the ratio of divorced persons was 47 per 1,000 married. By 1976 it had jumped almost 60 percent to 75 per 1,000.

While the Census Bureau study does not break down the marriage dissolutions* by race, it is obvious that the "divorce malady" does not affect only interracial couples. Although, to my knowledge, statistics about interracial marriages are not available, one can safely say that interracial unions represent an infinitesimal* percentage of the married population. Thus, the number of interracial divorces would not even be significant. What the statistics do indicate is a crumbling of traditional values, thereby affecting many facets of life, including marriage, divorce, child-bearing and child-rearing.

My marriage did not break down because of race. The cliché about social isolation resulting from interracial marriage did not hold. In Chicago I belonged to an interracial church. My friends included all kinds of people. Definitely this was enhanced by living in a neighborhood adjoining the University of Chicago. My four children had no problem finding playmates. The only trouble arose when my oldest son began attending a predominantly black elementary school and was derogatorily* called "mongrel." A similar incident was to be repeated in high school, this time in a predominantly white setting, with a racist white teacher referring to my son as "half-breed." But these hurdles were soon passed, and my children have made their own friends, including blacks, whites, and Orientals. Such experiences never became a serious problem in our lives.

My marriage broke down basically for two reasons. My ex-mate was a traditional wife who expected her husband to be the breadwinner and the disciplinarian. Moreover, the breadwinning should take place in the strict mold of a "9:00-to-5:00 job." Often my political activities required hours of bargaining, an activity that defies the strictures of time. When I intimated that inviting my friends or colleagues to my home would alleviate the situation, she quietly, but resolutely, opposed the idea. Eventually she confessed that she had kept the house messy so I would not be tempted to bring people home.

Then there was the matter of discipline. Increasingly I felt the estrangement between me and the children. They resented my coming home, and I cringed every time I was about to open the front door at night. Because, usually, their mother was waiting with a report detailing the misbehavior of this one and of that one. Appropriate punishment was in order, and it was my duty as father to mete it out. If the child had forgotten what he or she had done, it fell on me to offer a quick refresher course, before concluding with a growl, a spanking, or some kind of deprivation. The situation became unbearable, and I balked at being systematically typecast as an ogre.

Above all, our lives took opposite directions. I moved further away from what I perceived to be the hypocrisy of the organized church.

---

dissolution Context clue: "divorces."

infinitesimal Context clue: "not even significant."

derogatorily Context clue: The meaning of the passage indicates that the word must have a negative meaning.

Meanwhile, my ex-wife, together with some of my old friends and even my father, considered me as having "fallen from grace," that is, a sort of renegade to the faith. From their perspective, I needed to be "prayed for," so that I would eventually return to "the fold" where all believers belong. But I had other things in mind.

I began a career in journalism in 1970 and gradually built up a new life. I remarried in 1974—to yet another white woman. It should be obvious to all that I had had plenty of time to think about what I was doing in getting involved with another white woman. Exactly.

I had met my first mate in school. And my second at work. I am not one who feels that only "Black is beautiful" and "Whitey is the devil." Therefore, when it comes to finding a companion, I do not make a special trip to where "my own kind," whatever that means, are supposed to be. The way I look at human relationships, it is more a matter of social and cultural affinity, as well as proximity, rather than mere color of skin.

For some people, who are still going through identity crises, sticking to one's own kind may have meaning, yea, may be of utmost importance. But cultural and social compatibility is still more basic for a good marriage, be it intraracial or interracial.

In my present marriage, both of us have the same level of education, albeit in different fields. But I do understand and appreciate my wife's specialty, which is musicology. Besides being an afficionado* of classical music, I have developed a keen interest in the subject to the point of writing professionally about it. On the other hand, my wife has been of great help in my writing. She has become an editor of the English section of the *Haiti Observateur,* a French-language weekly newspaper I co-publish in New York with my brother.

I will point out that an interracial marriage, especially between individuals of different cultures, requires much more adaptability than the same marriage between individuals of the same culture. Thus, eventually black and white Americans should be able to get along better in an interracial situation than, say, a West Indian and an American would. Also, in an intercultural union, one of the two must be ready to accept more of the other's culture. In my case, I have been more adoptive of my wife's culture, for I live in the United States. However, if I were to be back in my own country, my mate would have had to be somewhat flexible to fit in the new milieu.

---

afficionado Context clues: "appreciate";
"have developed a keen interest."

Comprehension

These questions are to be answered orally or in writing. Some of them may require more than one sentence for your answer.

1. What information does the author give you about his father?
2. Why did the author become a revolutionary?
3. What is the reason that his parents left Haiti?
4. How does the author explain what he calls "the duality of Haitian culture"?
5. What was the author's reason for going to the United States?
6. What was his father's reaction to his decision?
7. What was the reaction of the missionaries to the author's plan?
8. How did the fact that the author is black influence the kind of advice he received?
9. What finally enabled the author to go to the United States to pursue his studies?
10. Joseph at first did not expect to graduate from the Moody Bible Institute. What enabled him to graduate?
11. What happened in 1960 that justified the author's reason for emigrating to the United States?
12. What happened in the author's personal life while he was at Moody?
13. Explain how Moody Bible Institute is hypocritical about its rule on interracial dating.
14. In what way was Joseph mistaken about Wheaton College's attitude toward interracial dating?
15. What happened when Joseph requested permission to marry Beth? (This question may require several sentences to answer.)
16. What happened when Joseph refused to sign a withdrawal card?
17. Was Joseph permitted to graduate? Describe exactly what happened with his finals and his degree.
18. What had happened to Joseph in 1955 that reminded him of his experiences at Wheaton?
19. What is the author's response to the idea that interracial marriages can't work?
20. Did his children encounter any incidents that scarred them emotionally? Explain your answer.
21. What are the two reasons that Joseph gives for the breakup of his marriage?
22. In what way did Joseph's and Beth's lives take opposite directions?
23. What does Joseph feel is most important in his relationship with his second wife, who is also white?

24. According to Joseph, why would an interracial marriage between a black American and a white American probably be more successful than one between a West Indian and an American?

25. What assumption about the duration of his second marriage does the author's concluding remarks seem to make?

DISCUSSION QUESTIONS

1. Discuss what happened to Joseph both at Moody and at Wheaton, first when he dated a white girl and later when he married her. How badly do you feel he was treated?

   The author worked out an agreement with Wheaton College regarding his examination and degree. Do you believe the agreement was biased? Generous? Fair? In view of Wheaton's code, "For Christ and His Kingdom," how was their attitude ironic?

2. This situation occurred over twenty years ago. Do you think it would happen anywhere today? Do you believe a school has the right to control the personal life of its students?

3. What is your opinion of mixed marriages? Have you ever dated a person of a different race? Of a different religion? Would you ever marry someone of a different race or religion? Why or why not? If you are already married to a person of a different race or religion, discusss your experience. Which do you think might be more difficult—marriage with someone of a different race or of a different religion?

4. Do you agree with the author's views on what is important in a marriage? Do you notice any inconsistency in his explanation as to why his second marriage is better? Does his second wife seem very different from his first?

5. Have you ever experienced discrimination of any kind? If so, relate the experience. What effect did the incident have on your view of yourself, on your attitude toward others, and on your religious or political beliefs?

6. Joseph was very active against the dictatorship in his native Haiti. Did you or any member of your family engage in any political activity in your own country? Discuss. Are you involved in the politics of your new country? If so, how? If not, why not?

CLOZE EXERCISE

Fill in each blank with a single (one) word.

        Beth and I fell _____ love. Our romance blossomed _____ the senior retreat, chaperoned _____ the deans, at _____ vacation ranch in Michigan in _____ fall of 1956.

We saw _____ other often that last _____ in school. It
was _____ open secret for many _____, but apparently no
one _____ the deans. I should _____ that besides my girl,
_____ year I had won _____ "most popular male senior
_____" by the secret ballots _____ the students.

Beth stayed _____ Moody for postgraduate work
_____ I went on _____ Wheaton—she wanted to accompany _____ Moody Chorale in their _____ of Europe in
the summer _____ 1958 and also worked _____ the Salvation Army. I _____ happy that now I _____ take my girl
to _____ school activities, for I _____ Wheaton more liberal _____ Moody. The dean soon called _____ in to
say that _____ "comportment" was "offensive" _____
some people. He admitted that _____ people he referred to
_____ the administration and some _____ the faculty.
At this _____ I lived with _____ white American family
that included _____ young children. They all _____
me and accepted Beth. _____ International Students had
voted _____ their president, and I _____ an officer of
_____ Anthropology Club. But I could _____ bring Beth
to _____ "Artists Series" _____ campus.

Vocabulary

WORD FORMS

Fill in the blanks with the correct forms of the word given for each group of
sentences. You may need the verb (changed where necessary for agreement
or tense), participles, a noun (singular or plural), an adjective, or an adverb.
Sometimes the form may require negative prefixes such as *un-*, *dis-*, or *in-*.

1. **oppose**

   a. The politician was asked why he _____ the views of the
   President.

b. Their plans to construct the building did not go through because of the _____ of the tenants.

c. Were the business firms _____ to the tax increase on their profits?

2. **tyrant**

a. She ran away from home because her father was a _____.

b. The nation revolted because of the persistent _____ imposed by the government officials.

c. Jailing political opponents is considered a _____ action in a democracy.

3. **convert**

a. His family was _____ to Catholicism only recently.

b. Thomas became a _____ to classical music when he was eighteen years old.

c. I checked the _____ rate of the dollar to the yen in the bank.

4. **assist**

a. The administrative _____ was asked to replace the boss for a few days.

b. Who is _____ the surgeon in the operation?

c. Most of the students need financial _____ to pay for tuition.

5. **withdraw**

a. The bank allows you to _____ money every month.

b. The psychologist concluded that George was a _____ child.

c. The war stopped as soon as the _____ of troops was announced.

6. **comment**

a. Did you have any _____ about the lectures on nutrition?

b. After the news broadcast, a short editorial _____ followed.

c. The director of the program _____ last week on the difficulty of the project.

7. **confirm**

a. After _____ the results of her experiments, she published an article on her work.

b. Catholics receive the sacrament of _____ when they are young.

c. I called the restaurant to _____ my dinner reservations which I made a week ago.

8. defy

a. The bureaucrats _____ all suggestions given by the public.

b. The _____ patients were released from the hospital because of the trouble they created.

c. The hostile students showed _____ when the school administrators talked to them.

9. resent

a. Mary _____ her being denied a job in school.

b. Nicolas is very _____ of his mother sending his brother overseas.

c. One could feel the _____ of foreign students toward incompetent teachers.

10. conciliate

a. John gave a _____ address after he found out that his workers were against him.

b. There was no _____ among the candidates concerning major issues.

c. The mediator hopes to _____ both sides in the strike.

11. crumble

a. The earthquake in Brazil _____ many fine buildings.

b. Some old, _____ bread was all they had to eat.

c. Do not offer me even a _____ of cake because I am too fat.

12. prolong

a. Her stay in Africa was _____ until the situation calmed down.

b. Every week he _____ the discussion long after business hours.

c. The _____ of Robert's business trip to California caused many problems for his firm.

13. interpret

a. We found it difficult to _____ the exact meaning of the document released by the Immigration Department.

b. The United Nations is always searching for qualified _____.

c. Every critic has a different _____ of the play.

14. **offend**

   a. To argue with a teacher is a big _____ in some countries.

   b. John was asked to leave the company because of his _____ attitude.

   c. Don't _____ Peter or he will kill you.

15. **expel**

   a. Patricio was _____ from school because he had a serious fight with the counselor.

   b. The x-rays show that the patient _____ a rather large tumor.

   c. The _____ of the foreign ambassadors created a scene in the United Nations.

SYNONYMS

Rewrite each sentence choosing an appropriate synonym from the list below for each underlined word or phrase.

1. affinity	6. ineligible	11. asset
2. hypocrisy	7. perspective	12. estrangement
3. proximity	8. controversy	13. dissolution
4. malady	9. vehement	14. encountered
5. verdict	10. outspoken	15. auspices

1. Many people were sick with a <u>disease</u> that was very difficult to cure.

_____

_____

2. The President of the United States has been very <u>frank</u> about the energy crisis.

_____

_____

3. Thomas was excommunicated because of his <u>strong and violent</u> denial of the church's teaching.

_____

_____

4. As a foreigner visiting a new land for the first time, Denise <u>confronted</u> language and racial problems.

_____

_____

5. Mr. Wang was assigned to work in Asia under the <u>support and protection</u> of the Institute of International Education.

_____

_____

6. Mary's knowledge of several languages was a <u>useful and valuable quality</u> when she applied for a job.

_____

_____

7. Students below the age of eighteen are <u>not qualified</u> for the driving exam.

_____

_____

8. The lawyer worked very hard to secure a <u>judgment</u> of not guilty for the poor girl.

_____

_____

9. Their friendship ended when <u>falseness</u> entered their relationship.

_____

_____

10. The issue of who should receive welfare checks is a constant <u>dispute</u> in the community.

_____

_____

11. In many cases, the <u>disintegration</u> of the modern family results from parents who are too busy with their own affairs.

_____

_____

12. Children from broken homes often experience <u>alienation</u> more as they grow up.

_____

_____

13. Because of the <u>closeness</u> of our homes, we became good friends in a short time.

_____

_____

14. According to my mother's <u>point of view</u>, I was not a dutiful child.

_____

_____

15. Our cultural <u>similarity</u> helped to keep our marriage successful.

_____

_____

Grammar

ABSTRACT NOUNS VERSUS VERBS AND ADJECTIVES

As you know from the word form exercises in this book and from your own experience of the English language, many abstract nouns are derived from adjectives and verbs. (Abstract nouns refer to ideas, concepts, or actions rather than concrete things or people.) In many cases, such nouns are formed by the addition of special endings (suffixes), which are mentioned below in Exercise A, although sometimes the noun is unchanged (for example, verb: to *increase*; noun: an *increase*).

Some writers tend to use more verbs and adjectives, believing that their writing is simpler yet stronger. Others rely more on abstract nouns to convey meaning. Thus, one person might write:

The director suggested enlarging the day-care center so that more children <u>could be accommodated</u>. (*verb*)

while another would prefer:

The director suggested enlarging the day-care center to provide for the <u>accommodation</u> of more children. (*noun*)

Probably the best writing maintains a balance of abstract nouns and verbs and adjectives. Such a balance will also provide more varied sentence structures and writing style.

GRAMMAR EXERCISES

A. Change these verbs and adjectives to nouns by adding an appropriate suffix from the following list:

(i)ty	ation	th
(it)ion	sion	al
ment	ness	ence

Other changes may also be necessary, such as omitting or adding a letter or two.

EXAMPLE
flexible (*adjective*): flexibility (*noun*)

Adjectives	*Nouns*
1. necessary	_____
2. strong	_____
3. happy	_____
4. confident	_____
5. safe	_____
6. lonely	_____
7. compatible	_____
8. adaptable	_____
9. equal	_____
10. warm	_____

Verbs	*Nouns*
11. agree	_____
12. announce	_____
13. oppose	_____
14. separate	_____
15. supervise	_____
16. argue	_____
17. permit	_____
18. dissolve	_____
19. attain	_____
20. suppose	_____

B. Rewrite each sentence using the noun form of the underlined adjective or verb, but keeping the general idea of the sentence. Many other words may have to be changed also. There will be more than one possible new sentence in each case.

EXAMPLES

My mate would have had to be somewhat <u>flexible</u> to fit in the new milieu. (*adj.*)

My mate would have needed some <u>flexibility</u> to fit in the new milieu. (*noun*)

My fiancé's parents <u>opposed</u> the marriage. (*verb*)

My fiancé's parents expressed <u>opposition</u> to the marriage. (*noun*)

1. My father finally <u>agreed</u> that I was doing the right thing.

_____

_____

2. The dean called me to his office to <u>announce</u> that the committee had turned me down.

_____

_____

3. When the dean <u>refused</u> to give me permission, I asked what would happen if I married without permission.

_____

_____

4. I refused, stating that I did not find it <u>necessary</u> to withdraw.

_____

_____

5. The answer was that skin color does <u>separate</u> people.

_____

_____

6. My wife <u>would supervise</u> me as I wrote my final examinations at home.

_____

_____

7. When I hinted that inviting my colleagues to my home <u>would alleviate</u> the situation, she opposed the idea.

_____

_____

8. The dean <u>argued</u> that the rules must be followed.

_____

_____

9. We believe that all races are <u>equal</u> before the law.

_____

_____

10. One must be very <u>strong</u> and <u>confident</u> to oppose the views of the majority.

_____

_____

C. Rewrite each sentence using the verb or adjective form of the underlined noun, but keeping the general idea of the sentence. Many other words may have to be changed also.

EXAMPLES

They were aware of my vehement <u>opposition</u> to the tyranny in my country. (*noun*)

They were aware that I vehemently <u>opposed</u> the tyranny in my country. (*verb*)

Many feared for the <u>safety</u> of my parents. (*noun*)

Many feared that my parents were not <u>safe</u>. (*adj.*)

1. To behave like "colonials" among the poor was the greatest <u>attainment</u> of the ruling class. (*verb*)

_____

_____

2. I will not give you the <u>satisfaction</u> of kicking myself out. (*verb or adj.*)

_____

_____

3. The Census Bureau study does not break down the marriage dissolution by race. (*verb*)

_____

_____

4. Increasingly I felt the estrangement between me and the children. (*adj.*)

_____

_____

5. Cultural and social compatibility is still more basic for a good marriage. (*adj.*)

_____

_____

6. An interracial marriage requires much more adaptability. (*adj.*)

_____

_____

7. It is evident that the child's loneliness was caused by being left back in school. (*adj.*)

_____

_____

8. The government will never give him permission to use human beings in his experiments to alter brain structure. (*verb*)

_____

_____

9. Why do you keep up the pretense that you are a wealthy person? (*verb*)

_____

_____

10. Many students were deceived by the simplicity of the questions and did not perceive their basic complexity. (*adj.*)

_____

_____

D. Write two sentences with essentially the same meaning, one using an adjective or verb, the other using its corresponding abstract noun.

EXAMPLES

verb: *to focus;* noun: *a focus*

In your essay, please <u>focus</u> on the problems, not the solution.   (*verb*)
In your essay, the problems, not the solution, should be your <u>focus</u>.   (*noun*)

adjective: *happy;* noun: *happiness*

How <u>happy</u> I could be if I had an interesting career.   (*adj.*)
What <u>happiness</u> I could have if I had an interesting career.   (*noun*)

1. curious, curiosity

_____

_____

_____

2. uncertain, uncertainty

_____

_____

_____

3. move, move

_____

_____

_____

4. obey, obedience

_____

_____

_____

5. warm, warmth

_____

_____

_____

6. repeat, repetition

_____

_____

_____

7. believe, belief

_____

_____

_____

8. cruel, cruelty

_____

_____

_____

9. interfere, interference

_____

_____

_____

10. depend, dependence

_____

_____

_____

SENTENCE COMBINING

Combine these sentences in the best way possible. You may find more than one possibility in most cases.

1a. My parents left Haiti.
  b. It was the year 1965.
  c. They never expected their visit to the United States.
  d. This visit would take them to the mission field.

_____

_____

_____

2a. They knew very little of my activities.
 b. My activities were revolutionary.
 c. They were aware of my vehement opposition.
 d. I was opposed to the tyranny in my country.

_____

_____

_____

3a. I was becoming more and more outspoken.
 b. I spoke against the tyrant.
 c. The tyrant was Haitian.
 d. Many feared for the safety of my parents.

_____

_____

_____

4a. I was nineteen.
 b. I began the first Christian print shop in South Haiti.
 c. This print shop was for the West Indies mission.
 d. The West Indies mission was an American faith mission.

_____

_____

_____

5a. The child had forgotten what he or she had done.
 b. It fell on me to offer a quick refresher course.
 c. This course was in good behavior.
 d. This course came before giving a spanking.

_____

_____

_____

6a. Later I spent one year in a little church back in the mountains.
 b. I gained much experience among Haiti's real people.
 c. These people are peasants.
 d. These peasants represent 85 percent of the population.

_____

_____

_____

7a. Our romance blossomed at the senior retreat.
 b. We were chaperoned by the deans.
 c. The retreat took place at a vacation ranch in Michigan.
 d. It happened in the fall of 1956.

_____

_____

_____

8a. I will never forget the pained look on the face of the dean.
 b. The dean was from Wheaton.
 c. I asked him if I could take Beth to a concert.
 d. The concert was at Orchestra Hall in Chicago.

_____

_____

_____

9a. The student newspaper published a caustic commentary on April 30, 1959.
 b. The commentary was about an idealistic young man.
 c. This young man came to the Land of the Free and the Home of the Brave.
 d. He was seeking an education, friends, and perhaps the answers to a riddle.

_____

_____

_____

10a. What the statistics do indicate is a crumbling of values.
  b. These values are traditional.
  c. These values affect many facets of life.
  d. These facets of life include marriage, divorce, child-bearing, and child-rearing.

_____

_____

_____

Writing Assignments

ESSAY TOPICS

Use at least three words from the vocabulary exercises. Remember to use words of transition where necessary.

1. Compare and contrast what the author calls the duality of Haitian culture and the duality of culture he found in the United States.
2. Write a character sketch of Mr. Joseph. Use as many of the details he himself has furnished as you can find. Suggestion: Before you begin writing, you might make a list of what seems admirable about him and what you find unadmirable or bad.
3. The author's stated views on interracial marriage are exceedingly revealing. What are your own views on interracial marriage? Do you agree with the author's views? Do you know of any interracial marriages that have been successful? If so, tell us why in your opinion this is the case. In other words, write an argumentative essay in favor of or opposed to interracial marriage.
4. Write an essay recounting an experience in which you or a person you know suffered discrimination. Describe the circumstances or background of the incident, the incident itself, and your reaction to it. What effect did the incident have on your view of yourself, on your attitude toward others, and on your religious or political beliefs?

PROOFREADING

There are 11 errors in the following passage. Find and correct them. Note: Run-ons (comma splices) and fragments each count as one error.

I don't opposed to the idea of getting married to a woman of a different race because love is what count when two people decide to marry. All human beings are created in the same way, their color or language may be different, but they have the same qualities. Many people think that because of better knowledge, more money, and their color make them superior to other races. I believe they do not. I don't believe in racism, and the person I marry have to be somebody who deserves my love. No matter what her color is. One important factor I want to point out is that the opinoins of others are not significant enough to stop me of marrying a woman of another race. If I and the person I love have decided to get married. We will do it even our parents are opposed to it. I will explain my parents and my friends that it is a decision I have to make myself.

CHAPTER 10

Assimilation

Our teacher showed us a newspaper story about Oriental women who had an operation to change their eyes because they wanted to look American.   I think that is ridiculous. I already feel like an American inside because I want to be a millionaire.   Isn't that what all Americans want?

From a Japanese student's paper.

READING PASSAGE

About the Author: Like many other middle-class Vietnamese, Anh-tuyet P. Le learned two other languages, French and English, in addition to her native Vietnamese.   Attending an elementary school in Paris for five years strengthened her proficiency in French.   Her ability in English also developed so well that she completed her B.A. in English literature at the University of California at Los Angeles and later received a certificate there in teaching English as a second language.   Mrs. Le worked as an English instructor and as a Foreign Service Officer in Saigon until she was forced to escape from her country in 1975 and returned to the United States as a refugee.

To Think About: As you read, try to answer the following questions.   (See page xiii for reading guidelines.)

1. According to the author, what do all immigrants or descendants of immigrants have in common?
   (Your answer will be the main idea of a paragraph.)

2. Ms. Le, the author, was first an immigrant to the United States.   How did she become a refugee, and what effect did her new experiences have on her feeling about her fellow refugees?
   (Your answer will be implications, supported by details.)

3. What does the author believe is the important difference between immigrants and refugees?
   (Your answer will be the main idea of the reading passage.)

4. What are some examples showing that the Vietnamese have a transient's mentality?
   (Your answer will be supporting details for a main idea.)

5. The author makes an interesting comparison of the melting pot metaphor and the salad bowl metaphor as applied to incoming immigrants and refugees.   Explain.
   (Your answer will be an implication.)

ASSIMILATION

ANHTUYET P. LE

"Look, my skin is yellow, my nose is flat, and my hair and eyes are black. I will never be an American," declared the middle-aged diminutive Vietnamese refugee in a defiant tone and with a slightly curved-lip grimace.* "After all," he added after a pause and a furtive glance toward people within hearing distance, "I did not come to the United States by free choice." Another pause. "Besides, who wants to be an American?" the man asked rhetorically.

The person is fictional, yet very real. The statement is no less fictional, yet very symbolical. I have met him and heard his profession of faith countless times. Of course, I do not share his frustration, but I could not help wondering about its cause.

In an effort to understand the problem, I will attempt to look into psychological facts that make a refugee different from an immigrant as well as into racial and cultural considerations behind such a negative attitude.

After graduation from high school in Saigon, I came to the University of California at Los Angeles in 1962 with a fresh, open mind. Like other foreign students, I had my share of trouble in the process of learning the English language and of adjusting to the American education, culture, and way of life. In getting to know my host country, I became increasingly interested in the multiracial* composition which makes this great nation of immigrants unique in the world. Many of my new acquaintances and friends were immigrants or descendants of immigrants. Unlike some native-born Americans who may take it for granted, all shared a common purpose, that is, the American Dream.* No matter where they had come from, all were praiseworthy for industriousness, thriftiness, and above all for their determination to make it* in America. Since they had left behind in the old countries whatever had prompted their departure for the New World, they were psychologically disposed to accept Americanization as the necessary step toward the fulfillment of their American Dream.

With my degree from UCLA, I returned to war-torn South Vietnam in

By permission of the author, Anhtuyet P. Le.

---

grimace   Context clue: ''curved-lip.''

multiracial   Context clue: the prefix *multi-*, meaning many.

the American Dream   The idea that every individual is capable of becoming a success, usually thought of in materialistic terms.

to make it   To succeed.

1970 and entered the Foreign Service. Not for long, because all of a sudden South Vietnam collapsed under the North Vietnamese onslaught in the spring of 1975. I escaped and made my way back to the United States, this time as one of the thousands of refugees flocking to this country. Among them were my grandparents, parents, sister, and scores of other relatives and friends. Then I became painfully aware of the refugees' plight.

As an old-timer, I gave a hand to my family and friends, while helping myself, in our struggle to resettle in the new land. In the process I became increasingly involved due to the nature of my responsibilities, first as a freshman job developer for the San Francisco Center for Southeast Asian Refugee Resettlement, and currently as a harried social worker for the Alameda County (California) Social Services Agency.

Over a two-year period, I worked with hundreds of refugees from all walks of life. What I suspected at first were isolated expressions of frustration on the part of the refugees began to fit together like pieces of a puzzle. These fell into a rough pattern that set the Vietnamese apart from the American mainstream as well as from other ethnic communities or political groups. My consciousness was focused on the refugees in terms of what makes them different from the immigrants.

While immigrants willingly come to the United States in search of a better future, refugees in general are reluctant newcomers who cannot get rid of their tormented memories of the tragic circumstances under which they left their countries and their past for an uncertain future. I may contend that the immigrants are refugees as well, in the sense that they fled poverty, persecution, or social injustice. The difference between the two groups lies in the fact that immigrants choose to leave their old countries and that refugees escape from theirs.

Once in the United States, the Vietnamese refugees manifest their reluctance in different ways, often disguised as unwarranted criticism against their hosts. Take this bespectacled former Saigon University professor who kept repeating that "Americans have no culture, not even a language of their own." Listen to this former college instructor who could not stand "the lack of education of American teachers."

"Americans have no class," complained the bejeweled wife of a former cabinet minister. An unwed mother living on welfare complained that "Americans are a cold, heartless people."

Unlike immigrants who expect a life of hardship before achieving the American Dream, many refugees adopt an unrealistic approach to life in America. Try to picture this classy* former prime minister who reported to a San Francisco field office of the California State Employment Development Department in the company of an aide, both wearing custom-tailored* business suits. Many others discovered the advantages offered by

---

classy Context clue: The base word is obviously *class.* Do you think it means high-class or low-class?

custom-tailored Made according to an individual customer's requirement, not mass-produced.

the welfare system, tried it, liked it, and got hooked* to its addicting side-effect.

Thanks to welfare, a former peasant would not join the stoop labor force in the San Joaquin Valley and would remain instead in the San Francisco crowd. An ex-Air Force pilot would request that employment "not below my former social status" be found for him.

The refugees from Vietnam in particular set a political precedent in the history of their host country. In general they tend to put the blame on the United States for allowing the defeat of their American-backed regime. The once idealistic politico-military involvement of the United States in Vietnam made its disengagement and the subsequent disaster all the more painful. "Here we are, the victims of U.S. intervention. You Americans ought to help us," a former politician would be heard thinking aloud.

Another problem is the way that the Vietnamese see themselves racially in regard to Americans. Before being more knowledgeable about the racial composition of the United States, I shared the simplistic view of other Vietnamese that most Americans were white, and some of them black. All others who did not fit into these two stereotypes were identified by their ancestry as Chinese, Japanese, Korean, etc. This mental refusal to identify fellow Asians as American was a psychological barrier or obstacle to the eventual absorption of the neither-white-nor-black Vietnamese into the mainstream. "I am not a white man. How can I be an American?" protested a former soldier.

While there is no such thing as an American race, there is definitely an American culture which, unfortunately, is sometimes misunderstood and somewhat looked down upon, due to its materialistic and individualistic overtone. Many a Vietnamese fears that this aggressive, young, and alien culture might wipe out a four-thousand-year-old Vietnamese heritage within the next generation. The Vietnamese are afraid that their children and descendants might not practice the sacred cult of their ancestors. They are afraid they might lose the respect due their elders as well as the spiritual understanding that holds their traditionally closeknit families together—just to name a few of the many cultural values which are apparently ignored by Americans. In the wake of a total defeat and following the loss of all worldly goods back home, the prospect of a losing battle to save a cultural heritage is scary indeed.

The last thing the Vietnamese want is to die and to be buried in a foreign land, which is the ultimate disgrace. Most adult Vietnamese consider their presence in the United States as temporary. They hope against all odds to return some day, somehow, to the land of their ancestors and to remain close to them in both life and death. Due to this transient's* mentality, they tend to stay aloof from American society. For lack of motivation, they hardly feel the urgent need to make any significant effort toward ac-

---

got hooked to   Became addicted to.

transient   Context clue: the meaning of the previous sentence (that the Vietnamese hope to return to Vietnam).

ceptance of the concept of Americanization. As a result, they hardly socialize with non-Vietnamese people, frown on mixed marriages, and live among, and with, themselves. They often remain prisoners in their own isolated world in which mental health problems multiply and worsen.

Thus we have the dramatic circumstances surrounding the escape of the Vietnamese from their home country, their political grievance against their host country, the nightmare of rebuilding their shattered lives in a racially and culturally alien society, and the fear of having their souls wander forever in a foreign land. I would contend that these factors may have contributed to the defiant, prideful attitude on the part of many of my fellow refugees toward our adopted country. Such an attitude denotes a feeling that is deep-rooted in their subconscious, that is, resistance to the onslaught of the Americanization process which inexorably sucks all newcomers, immigrants and refugees alike, into the all-powerful American melting pot, or salad bowl if you wish. The melting pot metaphor* would apply more readily to a mythical American population of all-European ancestry. I would opt for the more colorful and realistic salad bowl image, since the American society mixes races from all over the world which are actually not all that mixable.

Yet, I still feel optimistic as to the cultural integrity of the Vietnamese as an ethnic group in this country. They are the luckiest refugees who have ever been admitted into the United States, since all kinds of antidis-

---

melting pot metaphor The idea that all Americans of whatever origin melt, or blend, together to become the same. The image is taken from the pot in which metals are melted together and fused.

crimination laws and regulations are in force in their favor. In addition, the American consciousness is now at its peak in terms of racial and cultural mutual respect. I am confident that these favorable conditions, coupled with the Vietnamese resourceful instinct for survival, will assist the Vietnamese community's effort to preserve its own cultural heritage for generations to come. At the same time, these conditions will help the Vietnamese refugees to make the best of their unavoidable acculturation as full-fledged members of this great nation. My praise and respect at this point go to a former colleague of mine, a high-ranking official in the Foreign Service, who has taken a bank job as a security guard and gone back to school to learn accounting. I am certain that such people like him will make good,* and will make America all the greater.

. . .

Before concluding this attempt at dissecting the Vietnamese refugee's state of mind in the necessary adjustment and adaptation process, I should insert a cautionary note. The critical views expressed above are subjectively mine, given to bias, and may denote ignorance on my part. They are just disparate, yet repetitive, casual observations, and subsequent personal presumptions, made in the course of my counseling efforts as well as my services rendered other fellow refugees. I may add that they are not the result of any survey, research, study, or statistical computation. I assume that my experience in the field as a job developer and as a social worker may give credence to my views.

Anyway, being true to myself is already quite a feat. . . . Well, I leave the conclusion to you, my reader.

---

make good   Do well, succeed.

Comprehension

These questions are to be answered orally or in writing. Some of them may require more than one sentence for your answer.

1. Why does the middle-aged diminutive Vietnamese refugee say he will never be an American?
2. Why did he come to the United States in the first place?
3. What is a refugee?
4. What is an immigrant?
5. According to the author, what do all immigrants or descendants of immigrants have in common?
6. Why does the author believe that immigrants are psychologically disposed to accept Americanization?
7. Explain how the author, Ms. Anhtuyet Le, can be considered both an immigrant and a refugee.
8. When Ms. Le first began working with Vietnamese refugees, what was her original opinion of the frustration expressed by some individuals?
9. As Ms. Le worked with the refugees, how did she change her view of their expressions of frustration?
10. Both immigrants and refugees leave their native land because of conditions there. What are some of those conditions which are common to both groups?
11. What does the author believe is the important difference between immigrants and refugees?
12. What are some of the reactions Vietnamese refugees express about the United States?
13. What effect does the welfare system have on some of the refugees?
14. What sort of jobs does the average refugee want in this country?
15. What do South Vietnamese refugees say about America's role in their defeat?
16. What prevents the racial assimilation of the Vietnamese into the American mainstream?
17. What fears afflict the Vietnamese about their cultural values and their heritage, especially when it comes to their children?
18. What are some examples showing that the Vietnamese have a transient's mentality?
19. State, in your own words, the four factors that are important in the attitude of many Vietnamese refugees toward the United States.
20. What attitude have these factors produced?
21. What does the melting pot metaphor mean?
22. What does the salad bowl image mean?

23. Give at least two reasons for the author's optimism about the future of the Vietnamese refugees.

DISCUSSION QUESTIONS

1. Do you agree with the author's distinction between refugees and immigrants? What are your reasons for your opinion? Do you consider yourself to be an immigrant or a refugee? Have you yourself escaped from your native country or have you come here by free choice? Whichever group you yourself belong to, how much can you relate to the other group?

2. Do you agree with the author's comments about the immigrants' sharing of the American dream? What is your own definition of the American dream? Have you yourself (if your adopted country is the United States) adjusted to this dream? Explain your emotions or reactions at being a part of it. If your new country is not the United States, does it have its own dream? If it does, describe that dream and discuss whether it has also become your own.

3. How much do you relate to in the author's description of the fears of the refugees—fears of mixed marriage, fears of being buried in an alien land? Do you yourself feel any of these terrors? Do you have friends or relatives who suffer from them? Discuss how much you and your family and friends are fitting or trying to fit in the new culture in which you find yourselves.

4. Discuss the salad bowl metaphor as opposed to the melting pot image. Can either image be applied to the situation in the country where you are now living? If not, can you supply a more accurate image? Which image do you feel fits you?

5. Discuss some of the refugee examples that the author gives, such as the bejeweled wife and the former prime minister. How do these stories strike you? As pathetic? Ludicrous? Funny? Exaggerated? True to life? Do you know any similar stories of people who had unrealistic expectations of the kind of life they would live in their adopted country?

CLOZE EXERCISE

Fill in each blank with a single (one) word.

With my degree _____ UCLA, I returned _____

war-torn South Vietnam _____ 1970 and entered _____

Foreign Service. Not _____ long, because all _____

a sudden South _____ collapsed under the _____

Vietnamese onslaught in _____ spring of 1975. _____

escaped and made _____ way back to _____ United

States, this _____ as one of _____ thousands of

refugees _____ to this country. _____ them were my

_____, parents, sister, and scores _____ other

relatives and friends. _____ I became painfully aware

_____ the refugees' plight.

As _____ old-timer, I gave _____ hand to my family

_____ friends, while helping myself, _____ our struggle to

resettle _____ the new land. In _____ process I became

increasingly _____ due to the nature _____ my responsi-

bilities, first as _____ freshman job developer _____

the San Francisco Center _____ Southeast Asian Refugee

Resettlement, _____ currently as a harried _____

worker for _____ Alameda County _____

Services Agency.

Vocabulary

1. **symbol**

   a. The _____ of the United States is Uncle Sam.

   b. Her resignation was intended to be _____ of her resistance to the director's ideas.

   c. The dragon in Chinese history _____ power and wealth.

2. **psychology**

   a. One of my friends would like to major in _____.

   b. She could not get along with her colleagues because of _____ problems.

c. He stopped seeing the ＿＿＿＿＿＿＿＿＿＿ because it was too expensive.

3. **critic**

   a. Mary is open to all kinds of ＿＿＿＿＿＿＿＿＿＿.

   b. Edward was in a ＿＿＿＿＿＿＿＿＿＿ condition when the doctors operated on the malignancy in his colon.

   c. Before one ＿＿＿＿＿＿＿＿＿＿ the actions of others, one should look at oneself.

   d. Joanne received the award as the best ＿＿＿＿＿＿＿＿＿＿ of the year.

4. **intervene**

   a. Leon always ＿＿＿＿＿＿＿＿＿＿ in disputes between his friends.

   b. Egypt and Israel are discussing peace without the ＿＿＿＿＿＿＿＿＿＿ of the United States.

   c. The time ＿＿＿＿＿＿＿＿＿＿ between youth and old age passes too quickly.

5. **protest**

   a. The Palestinians ＿＿＿＿＿＿＿＿＿＿ the visit of the Egyptian President to Israel.

   b. In a ＿＿＿＿＿＿＿＿＿＿, there are often fights and bloodshed.

   c. The ＿＿＿＿＿＿＿＿＿＿ were taken to the county jail after a long struggle.

6. **material**

   a. What kind of ＿＿＿＿＿＿＿＿＿＿ did you use to make that beautiful dress?

   b. People have become ＿＿＿＿＿＿＿＿＿＿ due to the rapid changes in society.

   c. Professor Novack gave a lecture on "＿＿＿＿＿＿＿＿＿＿, Capitalism, and Socialism."

   d. The results of his reasearch may not ＿＿＿＿＿＿＿＿＿＿ for many years.

7. **dissect**

   a. Many people oppose the ＿＿＿＿＿＿＿＿＿＿ of animals even for scientific purposes.

   b. The Board of Directors ＿＿＿＿＿＿＿＿＿＿ the plan afterward to learn why it had failed.

   c. The biology and anatomy students were taught how to ＿＿＿＿＿＿＿＿＿＿ a frog in the first lesson.

8. **adapt**

   a. This book was ————————— from the Greek original.

   b. When John visited Hawaii last summer, he ————————— easily to the life-style he found there.

   c. The movie "79 Park Avenue" was an ————————— of the novel.

   d. Regina is more ————————— to new situations than Marianne.

9. **subjective**

   a. The judges in the contest were told not to be ————————— in their evaluation.

   b. Are you always aware when you are judging someone —————————?

   c. It is difficult to avoid ————————— in grading essays.

10. **repeat**

   a. Our new immigrants need a lot of ————————— in learning English.

   b. His writing is filled with boring and ————————— phrases.

   c. Don't ————————— what I just told you!

11. **counsel**

   a. The lawyer ————————— him to plead guilty.

   b. Their marriage ————————— finally advised them to separate.

   c. Many students need ————————— in job opportunities.

12. **survey**

   a. The architect ————————— the whole area before any construction was done.

   b. The Research Department did a ————————— on how many students commute to school everyday.

   c. She would like to become a ————————— for a mining company.

13. **compute**

   a. Calculators hasten the ————————— process but slow down the thinking process.

   b. Many math-oriented students tend to major in ————————— science.

   c. The Chinese ————————— figures by using the abacus.

14. **account**

   a. It's been ten years since Lucy has done any _____ work.

   b. The executive charged all his friends' purchases to his business

   _____.

   c. Because of her efficiency, Jane was considered the best _____ in the firm.

   d. Nowadays, one has to be _____ for every action that one undertakes.

   e. _____ has become an important issue in many schools.

15. **dispose**

   a. Bobby was known as a cheerful sort of man and very _____ to laughter.

   b. When the _____ of the estate has been agreed upon, the heirs will be quite wealthy.

   c. The manager of the department store is busy _____ of his business affairs so that he can take an early vacation.

SYNONYMS

Rewrite each sentence choosing an appropriate synonym from the list below for each underlined word or phrase.

1. disparate	6. harried	11. diminutive
2. stereotype	7. praiseworthy	12. nightmare
3. grievance	8. transient	13. disposition
4. heritage	9. disengagement	14. hooked
5. contend	10. optimism	15. subsequent to

1. The <u>tiny, small</u> man who stepped out energetically from the doctor's office was eighty-four years old.

_____

_____

2. All the participants in the pageant were <u>highly commendable</u> for their beauty, intelligence, and skills.

_____

_____

3. The public asked the Board of Directors for a discussion held <u>following</u> the meeting.

_____

_____

4. She had a lively, playful <u>temperament</u> which delighted everybody.

_____

_____

5. You <u>assert</u> that amnesty should be given to illegal aliens, no matter how <u>they</u> got into the country.

_____

_____

6. Today many juvenile delinquents are <u>attached</u> to alcohol instead of drugs.

_____

_____

7. The <u>detachment</u> of the United States from the Middle East Peace Treaty <u>made the</u> relationship between Egypt and Israel all the more valuable.

_____

_____

8. A <u>legacy</u> of affluence and position was transmitted from generation to generation in the Henderson family.

_____

_____

9. The <u>temporary</u> laborers were demanding equal payment for the farm produce that they harvested.

_____

_____

10. Under the Equal Rights Law, any <u>complaint</u> filed by the minorities should be given equal attention and <u>response</u>.

_____

_____

11. Many New Yorkers are experiencing the <u>fearful dream</u> of urban loneliness.

_____

_____

12. The very <u>conventional idea</u> of a college sophomore is an eighteen-year-old who is interested in sports.

_____

_____

13. During the war, the common people were <u>harassed</u> by the military officers whenever their orders were not <u>followed</u>.

_____

_____

14. My friend is a believer in philosophical <u>hopefulness</u>.

_____

_____

15. The <u>different and separate</u> factors involved in the tribal warfare were impossible to resolve.

_____

_____

Grammar

ABSTRACT NOUNS WITH EXPLANATORY CLAUSES

Abstract nouns often need explaining when they refer to ideas or concepts that exist only in the mind of the person using them. For example, in the sentence:

I shared the simplistic <u>view</u> of other Vietnamese.

the abstract noun, *view,* can have many meanings depending on the ideas in the mind of the writer. Sometimes, of course, the meaning is explained in another sentence. Very often, however, the meaning is given immediately in the same sentence.

EXAMPLE

I shared the simplistic view of other Vietnamese that <u>most Americans were white and some of them black</u>.

The explanation of the abstract noun takes the form of a complete clause connected to the sentence by the word *that.*

GRAMMAR EXERCISES

A. In these sentences, underline the abstract noun, circle the connecting word *that,* and underline the explanatory clause. (In one sentence note that there are two clauses explaining the noun.)

1. I have the feeling that you are unhappy.
2. I cannot forget the knowledge that the city was bombed by mistake.
3. Immigrants are refugees as well, in the sense that they fled poverty or persecution.
4. The committee has taken the position that last week's vote is invalid.
5. The difference between the two groups lies in the fact that immigrants choose to leave their old countries and that refugees escape from theirs.
6. Martha accepted the job only on the condition that she would have the same title as the men in the department.
7. Mr. Danda always lives with the fear that he may be deported.
8. Jeanne is willing to transfer to a smaller apartment with the understanding that she will pay less rent.

9. The alien was asked for proof that he had been legally admitted into this country.

10. Scientists long ago made the discovery that too much radiation is harmful to human beings.

B. Form sentences by matching a clause from the first column with a clause from the second and connecting the two clauses with *that*. In some cases, there may be more than one possibility for matching. For example, combine clauses 7 and J to form:

The minister will not change his opinion that gambling is not suitable for a church affair.

1. How many people still accept the cliche	A. a dam should not be built in this area.
2. I agree with the suggestion	B. he had not treated his friend fairly.
3. It is impossible to erase the idea from their minds	C. communism and democracy can coexist peacefully in the world.
4. The concept is relatively new	D. the building should be converted into a cooperative.
5. Another problem is the way	E. the Vietnamese see themselves racially in regard to Americans.
6. The union must agree to the condition	F. all the employees have to participate in the physical fitness program.
7. The minister will not change his opinion	G. no raises will be given for three years.
8. Motowe finally came to the realization	H. might makes right.
9. The tenants do not agree with the proposal	I. he was the murderer.
10. The manager submitted a recommendation	J. gambling is not suitable for a church affair.

1. _____

2. _____

3. _____

4. _____

5. _____

6. _____

7. _____

8. _____

9. _____

10. _____

C. Write sentences in which you use an abstract noun connected by **that** to an explanatory clause.

1. . . . the hope that . . .

_____

_____

2. . . . the discovery that . . .

_____

_____

3. . . . the position that . . .

_____

_____

4. . . . an agreement that . . .

_____

_____

5. . . . the proof that . . .

_____

_____

6. . . . the limitation that . . .

_____

_____

7. . . . the proposal that . . .

_____

_____

8. . . . the understanding that . . .

_____

_____

9. . . . the view that . . .

_____

_____

10. . . . the statement that . . .

_____

_____

SENTENCE COMBINING

Combine these sentences in the best way possible.   You may find more than one possibility in most cases.

1a. I graduated from high school in Saigon.
 b. I came to the University of California at Los Angeles.
 c. It was in 1962.
 d. I came with a fresh, open mind.

_____

_____

_____

2a. I was like other foreign students.
 b. I had my share of trouble in the process of learning the English language.
 c. I had my share of trouble in the process of adjusting to the American educational system.
 d. I had my share of trouble in the process of adjusting to the American culture and way of life.

_____

_____

_____

3a. They had left something behind in the old countries.
 b. This was whatever had prompted their departure for the New World.
 c. Therefore they were psychologically disposed to accept Americanization.
 d. This Americanization was the necessary step toward the fulfillment of their American dream.

_____

_____

_____

4a. I became increasingly involved.
 b. The reason was the nature of my responsibilities.
 c. I worked first as a freshman job developer.
 d. Currently I work as a harried social worker.

_____

_____

_____

5a. I try to picture this classy former prime minister.
 b. He reported to a San Francisco field office of the California State Employment Development Department.
 c. He was in the company of an aide.
 d. Both of them were wearing custom-tailored business suits.

_____

_____

_____

6a. Many others discovered the advantages offered by the welfare system.
 b. They tried it.
 c. They liked it.
 d. They got hooked to its addicting side-effects.

_____

_____

_____

7a. There is no such thing as an American race.
 b. There is definitely an American culture.
 c. This culture is unfortunately sometimes misunderstood.
 d. This culture is somewhat looked down upon, due to its materialistic and individualistic overtone.

_____

_____

_____

8a. They hardly socialize with non-Vietnamese people.

b. They frown on mixed marriages.

c. They live among themselves.

d. They often remain prisoners in their own isolated world in which mental health problems multiply and worsen.

_____

_____

_____

9a. My praise and respect at this point go to a former colleague of mine.

b. He is a high-ranking official in the Foreign Service.

c. He has taken a bank job as a security guard.

d. He has gone back to school to learn accounting.

_____

_____

_____

10a. Many a Vietnamese fears that this young culture might wipe out the Vietnamese heritage within the next generation.

b. This culture is aggressive.

c. This culture is alien.

d. The Vietnamese heritage is four-thousand years old.

_____

_____

_____

Writing Assignments

ESSAY TOPICS

Use at least three words from the vocabulary exercises. Remember to use words of transition where necessary.

1. Compare and contrast the immigrant's attitude toward acculturation and the refugee's attitude. As examples, use the experiences and attitudes of other people as well as your own. You may also use some of the material in the reading passages, expressed in your own words.

2. Write a paper about your own strong feelings concerning the culture of your former country. You might describe the way you still adhere to your own cultural mores, or, on the other hand, how you have adopted the customs of your present country. Perhaps your present situation is a combination of both, retaining some of your own culture while becoming assimilated.

3. From the facts given in the reading passage, the author is now a woman close to forty years of age, an experienced and thoughtful person. Does she strike you as the kind of woman you would find helpful as a friend? Why? What other personality characteristics can you discover about the author? Using the information given in the passage and your own inferences, write a personality or character sketch of the author.

PROOFREADING

There are 11 errors in the following passage. Find and correct them. Note: Run-ons (comma splices) and sentence fragments each count as one error.

The one in my family does not want to become an American is my older brother. He does not accept the fact that it was necessary for us to come to this country. He was an engineer in Hungary, where had a good position in a chemical factory. There was my father who insisted for our leaving because he could not bear the political situation. My brother was not interested in politics, he made enough money to start saving for a car, which was his main interest in life besides his job. Now he cannot get a job here until he took more courses to improve his English and to pass an engineering test. In the meantime, he is working as a waiter and is very unhappy. He just wishes he can be back in Hungary. On the other hand, I like it here very much. Especially because we have a larger apartment, and I share my room only with my brother instead of three people. Also, it is much more easier for me to meet other young people, I can talk to anyone I want without worrying about his politics beliefs.

CHAPTER 11

Cultural Differences in Nonverbal Communication

In this country, students don't even bother to stop talking when the teacher comes into the classroom. Many of them always come late. I still can't get used to it. In Ecuador, students stand up when the teacher enters. No one would dare to be late to class. It is a sign of disrespect.

From an Ecuadorian student's paper.

READING PASSAGE

About the Author: Carmen Judith Nine-Curt is a native Puerto Rican who came to the United States at seventeen to study at a university in Maryland.   There she won the English-language prize although Spanish was (and is) her native tongue.   She has devoted all her professional years as a university professor in Puerto Rico to improving the skills of Puerto Ricans and Anglos in communicating with each other.

To Think About: As you read, try to answer the following questions.   (See page xiii for reading guidelines.)

1. What forms of exchange make up communication between humans? (Your answers will be a paragraph's main ideas.)

2. Since communication forms usually become habits, which habits are the most difficult to change?   Give reasons for your opinions. (Your answer will be an implication, supported by details.)

3. What are at least three of the nonverbal methods of communication described? (Your answers will be the author's classifications.)

4. To achieve meaningful communication between two different cultures, must one culture change itself entirely to conform to the other?   Or, must both cultures make adjustments? (Your answer will be the main idea of the reading passage.)

CULTURAL DIFFERENCES IN NONVERBAL COMMUNICATION

CARMEN JUDITH NINE-CURT

Ray L. Birdwhistell, the famed American anthropologist, suggests that communication among humans is at most made up of only 35 percent verbal exchange. The rest, 65 percent, is nonverbal communication. Thus, for communication to take place between members of the same culture, both speakers and listeners have to be "in tune" to both the language and the nonverbal communication employed by each; otherwise, communication suffers, and we may not be able to understand what is being "said."

If communication within one and the same culture is possible because we understand the several levels at which it is taking place, what then of communication across cultures, where not only the linguistic system varies but also the nonverbal communication? We must agree that we have to study not only the language of the other culture, but also its nonverbal communication systems.

What are the behaviors classified as nonverbal?

First of all, in the field of *proxemics,* where space is studied, we find that the personal, uninvadable, nontransgressible distance at which you should stand away from somebody else in the United States among Anglos and in many other northern European countries is from 18 inches to 30 inches. Then, there is the intimate distance at which people also interrelate. In the United States, this distance is from skin contact to between 6 and 18 inches. This is culturally determined, a learned behavior, performed out of awareness day by day. However, it differs from culture to culture. How does space function in Puerto Rico and in many other countries of Latin America besides others in southern Europe? In Puerto Rico, personal distance is what is intimate distance in the United States, that is, from 6 to 18 inches. Thus, in dealing with Latins, many Americans feel that they want to spit because they find Latins too close, too pushy, and oftentimes, too "sexy." How do Latins feel when they talk to Americans and see them cringing back to regain, without their knowing, of course, their culturally learned comfortable distance? Americans seem aloof to us, cold, uninterested, or ... some may think ... prejudiced.

The above has always been an explosive area of interpersonal relationship between the two cultures; however, references to space have never

By permission of the author, Carmen Judith Nine-Curt.

been incorporated in the instruction in teaching English-as-a-Second-Language dialogues to our Puerto Rican students, nor in teaching Spanish dialogues to Anglos in Spanish-as-a-Second-Language classes.

Let us go into the field of *haptics* now, the field that studies touching. The United States and its Anglo world belong together with most northern European countries to noncontact, nontouching cultures. But the Puerto Ricans, together with most Latin Americans and Spaniards, are touching cultures. Puerto Ricans and most Latins touch to a degree that is outrageous and threatening, and oftentimes insulting to most Anglos. However, touching is a way of "talking" in most Latin countries. Take a normal everyday greeting among Mexicans, Puerto Ricans, Cubans, you name them. If you have already met, if you are friends or relatives, there is constant touching, slapping of backs, jabbing of the other person's body with finger and fist, kissing, and rubbing of bodies. If two women of the same age and social status meet, there is hugging, kissing and rubbing of the upper part of bodies, in some cases, and loads of shouting and screeching to express the joy and pleasure at meeting a dear friend. This might be considered "nutty" behavior, and definitely too exuberant for good manners among Anglos.

There are all kinds of nonverbal things involved and happening in even the simplest of greetings in all cultures and languages. In fact, greetings and leave-takings are one of the first kinds of dialogues to be learned in most English-as-a-Second-Language courses or foreign language courses. And this is right, for they are very important in language learning. However, they are very complex activities nonverbally speaking. When you try to greet in a different way from the one you learned in your culture, you feel extremely awkward, uncomfortable. We are culture bound,* for we have learned one way of behaving way back when we were small, and that is the "easy" and "right" way. Not only that, but we cannot shed it, anymore than we can shed our language or our eating habits. However, if culture is learned, then it can be taught. We should instruct our students in English-as-a-Second-Language and bilingual programs that if they are Latins they cannot go around over-squeezing Anglos, and Anglos should be taught that they should start squeezing their Latin friends—of the same sex, of course—if they do not want to be considered cold, unfriendly, rejecting, and sometimes outright insulting.

The next contrasting area between Anglo and Latin cultures is the way both cultures arrange their interpersonal relations. The United States is a monochronic culture, while Latin countries are polychronic. In the United States, most interpersonal relations, whether formal or informal, are carried out in a one-to-one sequence. If you go to a store, the clerk takes care of one person at a time. You form lines at windows, buffet suppers, most everywhere. I learned my lesson at Gimbel's, in New York City,

---

culture bound Limited to what one has learned
from one's culture.

when I interrupted a dialogue a clerk was having with a customer to ask her about some beads she had right in front of her. She snappily told me to wait for my turn. *Mono* (one) *chronic* (time)—one at a time. In Puerto Rico and other Latin countries, a clerk takes care of two, three, four people at a time. *Poly* (many) *chronic* (time)—many at a time. I have seen Americans depart in despair from a store counter in Puerto Rico and from friendly conversations because they insisted on waiting their turn or on speaking in a one-to-one order with their Latin friends. At the stores they tell the clerk they will wait their turn, when actually what they are doing is missing their turn completely.

Although shopping at stores is an important skill that any person living in the United States should master, now, with self-service stores, the problem has been reduced somewhat. Still, this contrast is an important one and should be included in our teaching, because the situation repeats itself not just at stores: polychronism is applied in all interpersonal relationships in Latin cultures. If I, as a Puerto Rican university professor, am talking to one of my colleagues or to one of my students, and another colleague of mine or student approaches me, wanting to talk to me, I immediately cease talking to the person I was talking to and acknowledge the newcomer. The other person I was talking to immediately ceases talking and lets the other person take his turn. In other words, and in contrast to American cultural ways, the newcomer has priority over the other person who was being taken care of or talked to. If a Latin is ignored when he approaches a friend who is talking to someone, he/she feels rejected and possibly hurt or insulted. In the United States, this same behavior is interpreted as lack of manners, as being rude. This is such a sensitive area in both cultures that the only way to solve the situation is by switching cultural channels* if we are in a culture different from our own. Puerto Ricans and other Latins must learn not to interrupt if they are in the United States; and Americans must learn to accept interruptions graciously when they are in Puerto Rico or in any other Latin American country.

The above also conditions the way we use our eyes. For example, people from polychronic cultures seem to have fan vision as opposed to tunnel vision, which seems prevalent among monochronic cultures. In other words, while a Latin talks to someone else, his eyes keep shifting from side to side, possibly in anticipation of newcomers. However, in talking to Americans, one must keep one's eyes on the person one is talking to. Actually this is somewhat difficult for a Latin to do and might give him/her cramps on the neck muscles. However, this is important. Shifting eyes sort of give a message of inattention or indifference to Americans, while a steady look may give a Latin a message of intimacy that Americans definitely do not want to convey.

Again, a steady look in the eyes of an older person makes a Puerto

---

switching cultural channels This is metaphorical language (see page 36). The author does not literally mean switching a TV channel. What *does* she mean?

Rican child brazen and disrespectful. However, when this same child avoids looking straight in the eye of his American teacher, the message is one of disinterest and disrespect. Actually, many a behavior in one culture may be considered pathological, sick in another. For this reason, the non-verbal communication of different cultures must be taught in our foreign and second language classes.

Oculisics is the name of the field that studies the way our eyes behave in interpersonal relationships. Here again we find another contrast between Puerto Rican and American nonverbal systems. A Puerto Rican woman will stare and smile at a strange woman in passing on the street. The absence of this stare and smile makes the world seem very lonely in the States for our womenfolk. There, it is not permissible to stare at anybody and much less smile. In fact, a very smiling American woman may be slightly insane, if not completely so. However, a Puerto Rican woman is not supposed to smile at a strange man, for the message is quite a different one from smiling at a strange woman. The American girl is allowed by her culture to be prodigal with her smiles (if she so wishes) with the opposite sex. Not so with Latin women. The message is quite different in both cultures. It is still culturally permissible for Puerto Rican men to stare at girls to their hearts' content and even drop complimentary comments on their passing. Girls cannot stare at men in Puerto Rico . . . as yet. But this might change, as so many other things are changing. The above behavior is totally impossible in the United States, for it would call the strongest reaction from an American woman, possibly even physical attack. What is considered nice, charming, playful in one culture is definitely insulting in the other.

Kinesics is the field that studies body motions and gestures. Puerto Ricans have possibly double the number of gestures that are used in the

United States, and some of them are completely strange to American eyes. However, they function quite widely in Puerto Rico, and everybody knows their meanings. Here are some examples:

Gesture	*Meanings*
1. Wiggling of nose with or without wrinkling of forehead.	What did you say? What is the matter? Is anything wrong?
2. Pointing with puckered lips at a person or object.	That one. Those there. Over there.
3. Moving finger from side to side.	No, no.

I believe it would be convenient for Puerto Ricans to remember that in order to relate better to Americans, they have to use words *besides* their gestures. If they use gestures alone, they run the risk of not being understood, or even of being considered rude.

Many more things could be added here regarding the nonverbal ways of communicating that both cultures consider normal, but there is not enough space to include everything. However, we might mention silence versus noise. To American ears, the tolerance for noise among Latins is incredible. Americans need silence to recharge their vitality, while for Latins nothing is better for feeling alive than lively talking, laughing, and kidding at the top of one's voice.

We could summarize what we have included above in the following fashion:

Latins	*NVC*	*Anglos*
1. Closer than for Anglos.	1. *Proxemics*	1. Farther apart than for Latins.
2. A touching culture.	2. *Haptics*	2. A nontouching culture.
3. Many at a time.	3. *Monochronism versus Polychronism*	3. One at a time.
4. Women stare at other women on street. Not much eye contact while talking.	4. *Oculisics*	4. No staring on street by anybody. More eye contact in talking to another person than in P.R.
5. More gestures and body movement.	5. *Kinesics*	5. Fewer gestures and rigid bodies in walking.

Comprehension

COMPREHENSION QUESTIONS

These questions are to be answered orally or in writing. Some of them may require more than one sentence for your answer.

1. According to Ray Birdwhistell, what does two-thirds of communication among humans consist of?

2. In order to communicate with a person from another culture with a different language, what should we study? (*Caution:* Keep in mind the *kind* of communication which we are studying.)

3. What are the two kinds of distance that the author discusses and how do they differ?

4. What is the distance that you should stand away from an Anglo whom you do not know very well?

5. Under what circumstances is it acceptable to stand four inches away from an Anglo?

6. In Latin countries, what distance is acceptable with a person whom you do not know very well?

7. What is a typical Anglo reaction when a Latin disregards his "non-transgressible distance"?

8. What does "touching" mean to a Latin?

9. Are Latin women allowed more freedom in their *touching* relationships with both sexes than are Anglo women?

10. When Latins greet each other, how much actual *touching* is part of the greeting? And in leave-takings?

11. In a store, what is the difference between monochronic and polychronic behavior?

12. Must a Latin remember this particular interpersonal difference when approaching a professor? Explain.

13. When two Anglos are in conversation, how does the field of oculisics function for them?

14. When a Latin woman stares or smiles at a Latin man, what message will she be conveying?

15. Will the use of such stares and smiles between two Latin women convey the same message or a different one?

16. Facial grimaces and finger motions convey messages from one Latin to another. Explain several of these nonverbal communications, first by *using* the gesture or motion; then by putting the action into words.

17. If you were to use the several gestures and facial expressions that you have just verbalized with an Anglo, instead of with a Latin, would that Anglo receive the message you intended? If not, what reaction do you suppose you would get from that Anglo?

18. What does an American need to replenish his energy?

19. How do Latins differ from Americans in their reaction to noise?

DISCUSSION QUESTIONS

1. In your own culture, what is the actual physical difference between "personal uninvadable nontransgressible distance" and "intimate distance"? How do these distances differ from the Anglo and Latin distance? If there are differences, how have you adjusted to them? Have these differences led you into any embarrassing situations? Explain.

2. What experiences have you had that relate to the field of haptics (touching)? What is the attitude toward touching in your culture? How does it differ from Anglo and Latin attitudes? If there are differences, how have you adjusted to them? What restraints have you imposed on yourself when greeting fellow students, teachers, neighbors, friends? Are these restraints the same with fellow students, with teachers, with neighbors, with friends? Have the differences between the two cultures led you into any embarrassing situations?

3. What is the difference in interpersonal relations between the Anglo and the Latin culture? Which culture is monochronic? Which culture is polychronic? Explain and discuss the way the monochronic differs from the polychronic. Have you had any embarrassing experiences because of the differences in interpersonal relations between the two cultures?

4. In the field of kinesics—body movements, gestures, and grimaces—what differences are there between your culture and Anglo cultures? Explain what the various gestures and grimaces in your culture represent. Discuss the Anglo's possible reactions at suddenly being exposed to this kind of nonverbal communication. Is it possible he may feel he is being insulted? Have your gestures ever been misunderstood? Have you found it necessary to change your gestures or grimaces?

5. With respect to oculisics, we find a big difference between the Latin and the Anglo culture. Explain what is meant by *fan vision*. Explain what is meant by *tunnel vision*. Which vision does your culture use? If you yourself have been accustomed to fan vision, do you find it embarrassing suddenly to use (or to attempt to use) tunnel vision when you are communicating with an Anglo? In moments of excitement, do you find yourself forgetting the restraints you have been trying to learn? Do you find it then almost impossible to repress that spontaneous flash of the eye? Have you found yourself in embarrassing situations because of the radical differences between the two cultures in this particular field?

6. What is the difference between the Latin and the Anglo cultures with respect to noise? What is the Latin use of noise? What is the Latin's reaction to others' use of noise? What is the Anglo's reaction both to his own "use" of noise and to the use of noise by others? Try to explain

these differences. Also, if you can, try to explain why the one culture thrives on noise and the other one shrinks from it. What is your own culture's attitude towards noise? Have you found yourself in any embarrassing situations because of noisy communication with another culture?

7. Have you ever had instruction in nonverbal communication in your English class? If so, what did you learn from it? Were you able to change some of the ways you were used to in nonverbal communication? If you never received such instruction, do you feel that it would have made your life easier in your new country if you had? If you were not previously instructed, do you feel resentful?

CLOZE EXERCISE

Fill in each blank with a single (one) word.

Although shopping at stores _____ an important skill that _____ person living in the _____ States should master, now, _____ self-service stores, the problem _____ been reduced somewhat. Still, _____ contrast is an important _____ and should be included _____ our teaching, because the _____ repeats itself not just _____ stores: Polychronism is applied _____ all interpersonal relationships _____ Latin cultures. If I, _____ a Puerto Rican university professor, _____ talking to one of _____ colleagues or to one _____ my students, and another colleague _____ mine or student _____ me, wanting to talk _____ me, I immediately cease _____ to the person I _____ talking to and acknowledge _____ newcomer. The other person _____ was talking to immediately _____ talking and lets the _____ person take his turn. _____ other words, and in _____ to American cultural ways, _____ newcomer has priority over _____ other person who was _____ taken care of or _____ to. If a Latin _____ ignored when he approaches _____ friend who is talking _____ someone, he/she feels rejected _____ possibly hurt or insulted. _____ the

United States, this _____ behavior is interpreted as _____ of manners, as being _____. This is such a _____ area in both cultures _____ the only way to _____ the situation is by _____ cultural channels if we _____ in a culture different _____ our own. Puerto Ricans _____ other Latins must learn _____ to interrupt if they _____ in the United States; _____ Americans must learn _____ accept interruptions graciously when they _____ in Puerto Rico or _____ any other Latin American _____.

Vocabulary

WORD FORMS

Fill in the blanks with the correct forms of the word given for each group of sentences. You may need the verb (changed where necessary for agreement or tense), participles, a noun (singular or plural), an adjective, or an adverb. Sometimes the form may require negative prefixes such as *un-*, *dis-*, or *in-*.

1. **communicate**

   a. It was difficult to maintain _____ during the blackout.

   b. Do you _____ often with your aunt in Japan?

   c. Mononucleosis is a _____ disease.

   d. The scientist was not very _____ about his new research.

2. **culture**

   a. Is it possible to preserve one's ethnic _____ in a foreign land?

   b. Whether or not women go out to work is usually _____ determined.

   c. New York, Paris, and London are three great _____ centers of the Western world.

3. **personal**

   a. Robert is one of my _____ friends.

   b. Are you _____ acquainted with any famous people?

c. I am still a _____ with feelings and emotions.

d. A good supervisor is one who can _____ her relationships while maintaining discipline.

4. **determine**

a. Because of her strong _____, Jane was able to get to the top in her firm.

b. Lucy was so _____ to study in France.

c. How does one _____ whether to eat Vienna sausage or a hamburger sandwich?

5. **distant**

a. The _____ between Palmillas and Querétero, Mexico is about 40½ miles.

b. Their new house seems so _____ from shopping and other conveniences.

c. Her manner was so _____ that I hesitated to ask a question.

6. **prejudice**

a. Many countries are still trying to eliminate _____ against minorities.

b. She is so _____ that it is impossible to discuss any issues with her.

c. During a court trial, jurors are not allowed to read any literature _____ to the case.

7. **instruct**

a. English is the medium of _____ in many countries.

b. The math _____ was invited to give a lecture-forum.

c. The coach _____ the players to watch out for dirty tricks from their opponents.

8. **insult**

a. The customer _____ the manager when he refused to exchange the merchandise.

b. Her comments about his accent were _____.

c. His rudeness was an _____ to the visitors.

9. **behave**

   a. His _____ is very disturbing.

   b. He is _____ very strangely because he is ill.

   c. In order to _____ correctly in all situations, one must possess a thorough knowledge of etiquette.

   d. Their _____ problems were so severe that no one could control them.

10. **contrast**

   a. Tim's verbosity is in _____ to Ingrid's reticence.

   b. The brightness of the TV _____ unpleasantly with the darkness of the room.

   c. I need a _____ color to make the outfit more interesting.

11. **acknowledge**

   a. We _____ your superior knowledge in this matter.

   b. The publisher requested the author to write an _____ of the help he had received.

   c. It is an _____ fact that the more skills one possesses, the more opportunities one has.

12. **reject**

   a. I totally _____ your offer of a free trip to Asia.

   b. My friend was _____ for admission to medical school.

   c. She was greatly hurt by her friend's _____.

13. **despair**

   a. He began to _____ after having written eight sentences.

   b. In _____, the boy wrote down whatever came to mind.

   c. It was a _____ man who continued to gamble in the casino.

14. **refer**

   a. The plans to which you _____ will soon be back in our hands.

   b. In her job application, she was asked to supply several _____.

   c. Were you _____ to that gentleman in the blue shirt?

15. **suffer**

a. He _____ from a most unusual malady.

b. My father was _____ from pneumonia before he died.

c. The _____ of war victims is too soon forgotten after a war.

SYNONYMS

Rewrite each sentence choosing an appropriate synonym from the list below for each underlined word or phrase.

1. conveyed	6. sensitive	11. gestures
2. bilingual	7. anticipation	12. prevalent
3. priority	8. interrelate	13. incorporated
4. contrast	9. exuberant	14. jabbed
5. sequence	10. awareness	15. shed

1. Applicants who are able to speak two languages with equal skill have more opportunities in the job market nowadays.

_____

_____

2. The engineers wanted to show the differences between the new and the old buildings to the construction company.

_____

_____

3. It was difficult for the patient and the doctor to establish a mutual relationship with one another because the patient's feelings were hurt.

_____

_____

4. One reason why students have difficulty in writing is the lack of consciousness about their own ideas.

_____

_____

5. The staff from the branch office was combined with that from the main office because of the budget crisis.

_____

_____

6. Peter poked his elbow into his friend's side to get his attention.

_____

_____

7. Lisa felt joyous upon learning that she had won the lottery.

_____

_____

8. Some animals take off their fur once a year.

_____

_____

9. In some colleges, all courses must be taken in a particular order.

_____

_____

10. The President announced that the issue of human rights will be given the greatest importance in his program.

_____

_____

11. Offering a seat to a woman does not seem common among big city dwellers.

_____

_____

12. The expectation of her long lost friend's arrival made her very nervous.

_____

_____

13. We all rely more than we realize on expressive movements of the face and body to communicate with others.

_____

_____

14. Increasing unemployment is a touchy and delicate issue between the government and the workers.

_____

_____

15. Their mother's quick recovery <u>transmitted</u> a sense of hope to the entire family.

Grammar

WORDS OF TRANSITION II

In chapter 6, we saw that words of transition help the writer move smoothly from one idea to another. They serve as cues or signals to the reader about the kind of relationship the writer wants to establish between ideas. Thus, we examined such relationships as emphasis; the addition of one idea to another; and the ordering of ideas according to importance, time, and space.

Look back at the previous paragraph and underline a word of transition that does *not* fall into any of the categories just mentioned. You will find it in one of the groups below.

Relationship Between Ideas	Words of Transition
Emphasis	in fact, indeed, certainly, again, undoubtedly, surely, truly, to repeat, actually
Addition	in addition, also, moreover, furthermore, too, again
Ordering according to importance	more important, most important, first, second, third, next, last, finally
Ordering according to time	next, then, now, immediately, soon, before, after, meanwhile, gradually, finally, suddenly, previously, subsequently, in the meantime, yesterday, today, tomorrow, just, already, at last, first, second, when
Ordering according to space	below, above, under, beyond, near, far, in front of, to the right, to the left, around, on one side, inside, outside, in back of, across
Giving examples	for example, for instance, as an illustration, specifically

Comparison	likewise, similarly, in the same way, just as
Contrast	however, but, still, nevertheless, although, even though, on the other hand, on the contrary, in contrast, in spite of, yet, despite
Cause and effect	therefore, thus, then, accordingly, consequently, because, since, as a result, hence, so
Purpose	for this reason, for this purpose
Summary	in other words, in brief, in conclusion, in summary, finally, on the whole, to sum up, as I have shown

GRAMMAR EXERCISES

A. Using the chart, explain orally why the underlined words have been used as transitions in this paragraph.

What are the behaviors classified as nonverbal? <u>First of all</u>, in the field of *proxemics*, where space is studied, we find that the personal uninvadable, nontransgressible distance at which you should stand away from Anglos in the United States and in many other northern European countries is from 18 to 30 inches. <u>Then</u>, there is the intimate distance at which people <u>also</u> interrelate. In the United States, this distance is from skin contact to between 6 and 18 inches. This is culturally determined, a learned behavior. <u>However</u>, it differs from culture to culture. In Puerto Rico, personal distance is what is intimate distance in the United States, that is, from 6 to 18 inches. <u>Thus</u>, in dealing with Latins, many Americans feel that they want to spit because they find Latins too close.

B. Underline all transition words in one or two pages of the reading passage and explain orally how they are being used.

C. Fill in the blanks with an appropriate word or phrase of transition. Try to use different words from each group.

1. A Puerto Rican woman will smile at a strange woman in passing on the street. The absence of this smile makes the world seem very lonely in the United States.

   (*space*)————————————————, it is not permissible to smile at anybody.   (*emphasis*)

   ————————————————, a very smiling American woman may be considered slightly insane.

2. People from polychronic cultures seem to have fan vision as opposed to tunnel vision, which seems prevalent among monochronic cultures. *(example)* _____, while a Latin talks to someone else, his eyes keep shifting from side to side. *(contrast)* _____, in talking to Americans, one must keep one's eyes on the person one is talking to.

3. There are all kinds of nonverbal behavior involved in even the simplest of greetings in all cultures and languages. *(emphasis)* _____, greetings are one of the first kinds of dialogues to be learned in foreign language courses.

4. Psychologists say that the first five years of a person's life are extremely important to emotional development. *(cause and effect)* _____ a happy childhood might mean a more stable personality as an adult.

5. When my family travels, what we enjoy seeing most are natural wonders. *(example)* _____, the Alps in Switzerland and Glacier National Park in Montana have some of our favorite scenery.

6. Many plants grow best in a tropical climate. *(purpose)* _____, you should keep the heat and a humidifier going all the time in your apartment.

7. Ostriches are known to put their heads in the sand, believing that their entire bodies are hidden. *(comparison)* _____, very young children often close their eyes thinking that no one can see them.

8. In planning our camping trip, we found that our needs often conflicted with each other. *(example)* _____, we wanted our packs to be as light as possible. *(contrast)* _____, we all like to eat big meals which would mean carrying a lot of food. *(addition)* _____, we prefer fresh vegetables and meat to the dried, but lighter-weight products. *(cause and effect)* _____, we had to decide between heavy packs and unappetizing meals.

D. Fill in the blanks with an appropriate word or phrase of transition. In this exercise you yourself will decide what kind of transition word is needed, since the groups are not indicated.

1. A steady look in the eyes of an older person makes a Puerto Rican child brazen and disrespectful. _____, when this same child avoids looking straight in the eye of his American teacher, the message is one of disinterest and disrespect. _____, many a behavior in one culture may be considered pathological, sick in another. _____, the nonverbal communication of different cultures must be taught in our foreign and second-language classes.

2. The women's movement has made some progress in many parts of the world.

_____, not all the results have been good. _____, in some countries, men are afraid that there will not be enough jobs if all women work. Men want to continue having the advantage of better jobs and higher pay.

_____, some men are glad their wives are able to share the heavy responsibility of earning a living for a family.

3. Building your own house is a great challenge, for you must acquire many mechanical skills.

_____, you have to know something about the proper materials,

their costs, and where you can buy them. _____, building a house is a difficult job for an amateur.

4. The ship sailed at noon, two hours late, although a very important passenger had not yet

arrived. The crew was not surprised, _____, when a telephone message came through insisting that the ship stop and wait for the passenger to arrive by heli-

copter. _____, the other passengers could not believe it when they heard that it was the captain who had been left behind!

SENTENCE COMBINING

Combine these sentences in the best way possible.   You may find more than one possibility in most cases.

1a. Two women of the same age and social status meet.
 b. There is hugging, kissing, and rubbing of the upper part of the bodies.
 c. There is loads of shouting and screeching.
 d. This shouting and screeching expresses the joy and pleasure at meeting a dear friend.

_____

_____

_____

2a. You try to greet someone in a different way.
 b. This way is different from the one you learned in your culture.
 c. You feel extremely awkward.
 d. You feel extremely uncomfortable.

_____

_____

_____

3a. I learned my lesson at Gimbels.
 b. Gimbels is in New York City.
 c. I interrupted a dialogue a clerk was having with a customer.
 d. I asked her about some beads she had right in front of her.

_____

_____

_____

4a. I have seen Americans depart in despair from a store counter in Puerto Rico.
 b. They insisted on speaking in a one-to-one order with their Latin friends.
 c. I have seen Americans depart from friendly conversations.
 d. They insisted on waiting their turn.

_____

_____

_____

5a. Shopping at stores is an important skill that any person should master.
 b. This person lives in the United States.
 c. The problem has been reduced somewhat now.
 d. There are many self-service stores.

_____

_____

_____

6a. I am talking to one of my colleagues and another colleague wants to talk to me.
 b. I am a Puerto Rican university professor.
 c. I immediately cease talking to the person I was talking to.
 d. I immediately acknowledge the newcomer.

_____

_____

_____

7a. A Latin is ignored when he approaches a friend.
   b. The friend is talking to someone.
   c. The Latin feels rejected.
   d. The Latin possibly feels hurt or insulted.

_____

_____

_____

8a. Puerto Ricans and other Latins must learn not to interrupt.
   b. They are in the United States.
   c. Americans must learn to accept interruptions graciously.
   d. They are in Puerto Rico or in any other Latin American country.

_____

_____

_____

9a. Shifting eyes sort of give a message of inattention.
   b. Shifting eyes sort of give a message of indifference to Americans.
   c. A steady look on you may give a Latin a message of intimacy.
   d. Americans definitely do not want to convey this intimacy.

_____

_____

_____

10a. They use gestures alone.
    b. They run a risk.
    c. This risk is not being understood.
    d. This risk is also being considered rude.

_____

_____

_____

Writing Assignments

ESSAY TOPICS

Use at least three words from the vocabulary exercises. Remember to use words of transition where necessary.

1. Compare and contrast the nonverbal communication practices you grew up with and those practiced by another culture. Show similarities, if you find any, as well as differences.

2. Analyze your own personal problems in overcoming the habits you acquired in your own culture. Explain what help (or lack of help) you received in so doing. In this analysis, please explain which of these new nonverbal methods you liked the most, or disliked the most, as the case may be. Also, be sure to state which one has been the most difficult for you to acquire and which one was the easiest. You might also state which habit from your own culture you most regretted having to discard or to unlearn.

3. Write an essay describing your first encounter with a person or group of persons of a different culture from yours. Be sure you compare and contrast the way *you* reacted to them, as well as the way *they* reacted to you.

4. Write an argumentative essay in favor of or in opposition to changing one's habits in nonverbal communication. Describe the kind of compromise you would consider ideal, or at least workable. In other words, if you are Latin, perhaps you feel strongly that the Anglo should change entirely over to your ways. Do you feel it is not right for you to make all the adjustments in the Anglo's world? Keep in mind the question of flexibility. Does the Anglo pride himself on his flexibility? If so, let him demonstrate it! (That could be a point.) But, if you feel that the Latin is more flexible than the Anglo, this superiority in the art of adjustment—for adjustment is, indeed, an art—should make you more tolerant in dealing with the other culture. Try very hard to state both sides of the argument. Put yourself in the place of the person of the other culture.

PROOFREADING

There are 7 errors in the following passage. Find and correct them. Note: Run-ons (comma splices) and sentence fragments each count as one error.

Once I was walking with an American friend along the Bowery.

When we saw two Chinese men walking with their arms around each others' neck. My American friend insisted that those men were gay. I told him that he is wrong, explaining what I meant. According to Chinese custom, if two men are really good friends, they will often put their arms around each other, they consider this a sign of normal friendship. Chinese men are not afraid to show feeling for another man in public. My American friend said that although he understood, but he would rather not put his arm around a friend's neck; it would be misinterpreted by his people. In United States today, men have to be careful how they act with other men because unfortunatly people are very concerned about homosexuality.

Appendix

Corrected Proofreading
Passages

Corrected words, phrases, punctuation, and capitalization, as well as inserted words, have been underlined. Where it was necessary to omit a word in the corrected version, the spot is indicated by underlining between the two adjacent words.

CHAPTER 1: Page 21

My trip to the United States actually started five years before I arrived there. In my country, the Dominican Republic, we were told by our friends that life in the United States would be difficult because* we did not know English. My family decided to go to Puerto Rico where Spanish was spoken. However, after four years, we realized that our chances for success were not very great. Therefore, we decided to go to the United States mainland. First, we studied English for a year to make life easier when we arrived. When we finally reached New York, the airplane trip seemed very short compared with the five years since we had left our own country.

CHAPTER 2: Page 44

My first week in America was one of the most interesting weeks I have ever lived through. I was assigned to a nearby high school where I found that I wasn't the only non-English-speaking student. Unfortunately, none of my new classmates spoke my native language. However, I began to make progress in English immediately. After school every day, a friend took me sightseeing. The shopping centers were very impressive, and the number of movies and theaters was overwhelming. There were also a few things that disappointed me. One of them was the subway, which seemed to be the worst in the world. Another very disturbing thing was the poor condition of many neighborhoods. I didn't expect to see so many of them in such bad shape.

CHAPTER 3: Page 67

The ability to acquire English depends to a great extent on the background of the family. When I was eleven years old, I was very eager to

* Note that the comma splice here has been corrected by inserting a conjunction, because.

learn English. I was <u>helped</u> by my father, who taught me how to pronounce and spell words. As the years <u>went</u> on, I could read a lot and increased my vocabulary. When I finished <u>high</u> school, I insisted
<u>on entering</u> a college that used English as the main language. There,
I <u>learned</u> how to use proper English in reading and <u>writing</u>. Above all, I
learned <u>thousands</u> of medical terms.

When I came to this country, I could understand everyone very well.
I tried and <u>am</u> still trying very hard to improve my English. At the beginning, I could not read the newspaper because it had a lot of <u>abbreviations</u>
and difficult words, but after <u>a</u> few months, I learned by myself how to
read the newspaper, and now I enjoy <u>reading</u> any article.

CHAPTER 4: Page 91

I looked for a job because I had to help my family. My sister said <u>she</u>
would talk to her sister-in-law, who was the Executive Assistant at Coney
Island Hospital. I filed an application for <u>the</u> position of Ward Clerk.

I got the job. <u>Before</u> I started working, my supervisor told me to be
there for one day to familiarize <u>myself</u> with the work. The first thing I had
to do every morning was to prepare the lab slips so that when the <u>techni-
cians</u> came to draw blood from the patients, they <u>would</u> know what type of
test was <u>needed</u>. I had to answer <u>the</u> telephone, order supplies, and <u>enter</u>
the test results on the charts of the patients.

People were very nice to me, and I enjoyed working with the <u>pa-
tients</u>. My supervisor told me that I was the first clerk <u>who</u> did her work so
<u>well. However</u>, I was afraid of losing my job. Soon the city didn't have
enough money, so I <u>was</u> laid off.

CHAPTER 5: Page 112

I live <u>on</u> the west side of Manhattan. <u>Across</u> the street from my house
is the junior high school that I <u>used</u> to attend. On the block, there are
many old <u>buildings</u> that seem to be falling down. There <u>are</u> also a super-
market, a <u>barber</u> shop, three restaurants, a Chinese laundry, and a fire-

house. During the daytime, the street is filled with children from the school. At night, many rich, high-class people drive around in their big Cadillacs and Mercedes-Benzes and look for parking spaces. That is because they are going to all the theaters and playhouses that are located in the area. I like the neighborhood, but I am a little ashamed to tell people where I live. Everyone knows that the area is full of prostitutes. Although I don't mind living here right now, I wouldn't want to stay here forever.

CHAPTER 6: Page 134

As a Haitian who has studied in Haiti for many years and who is studying now in the United States, I find that the Haitian and American educational systems are quite different from each other. What are their differences?

The first remark I would make is that in American schools the student can choose among different options offered in one subject. This freedom does not exist in the Haitian curriculum. Although Haitian schools have different sections, such as A (Humanities), B (Languages), and C (Science), only some famous private schools offer the C section. The Haitian is thus used to following a rigid course distribution, and personally, I have been surprised by the freedom of choice given in the American system.

In Haiti, the student never has multiple-choice tests or true-or-false questions. He is also exposed to a very strict grading system where one almost never gets 100, even if one deserves it. On the other hand, the passing grade is 50. Thus my transcripts, if they have not been adjusted to American standards, might look very poor when in reality they are not bad.

CHAPTER 7: Page 158

My friend would probably never have told me that he was here illegally, but one day I asked him to go with me to fill out some papers. I wanted him to interpret for me if I did not understand the questions. He said he could not go because he was afraid someone would find out that he had no immigration papers. It was impossible for me to hide my curiosity, so I asked him how he had come to this country. He said many people go to Puerto Rico. Then they just fly to New York. Since Puerto Ricans are Americans, no one asks passengers from Puerto Rico for identification. My friend told me that he came first with his father. Afterwards his mother came with his sisters. They were very poor in their own country and believed life would be better here. At first, they were always afraid that the police would arrest them, but nobody asked any questions, not even their bosses. Now they don't worry too much, but they avoid going near an immigration office.

CHAPTER 8: Page 182

I will not commit the fallacy of attacking the author, yet many paragraphs of that passage revealed inconsistencies. It was an unfortunate event for her to be caught in the world of power politics. She must have realized that she had nothing to do with her country's aggression, but because of her loyalty, she presented contradictions for herself instead of upholding her integrity. She explained that even if Japan was the aggressor, she was merely defending her legitimate interests. I thought it was really naive for her to utter those statements. At least, she didn't make any apology for Japanese brutality. Otherwise she would have seemed hypocritical. Still, "modern warfare" is no excuse for brutality. Most people can sense what is a brutal act. I doubt very much that brutality can be wiped away so casually.

When I was in Japan, I visited the War Museum of Nagasaki. It is a four-story building near the atom-bomb site. Inside it pictures and remains are exhibited which are a thousand times more horrible than what the author had seen in Geneva. I personally felt those kinds of destruction were awful, and naturally I wondered why the American Armed Forces used a cannon to shoot a mouse.

CHAPTER 9: Page 207

I <u>am</u> <u>not</u> opposed to the idea of getting married to a woman of a different race because love is what <u>counts</u> when two people decide to marry. All human beings are created in the same wa<u>y. T</u>heir color or language may be different, but they have the same qualities. Many people think tha<u>t b</u>etter knowledge, more money, and their color make them superior to other races. I believe they do not. I don't believe in racism, and the person I marry <u>has</u> to be somebody who deserves my love<u>, no</u> matter what her color is. One important factor I want to point out is that the <u>opinions</u> of others are not significant enough to stop me <u>from</u> marrying a woman of another race. If I and the person I love have decided to get marrie<u>d, we</u> will do it even <u>if </u>our parents are opposed to it. I will explain <u>to</u> my parents and my friends that it is a decision I have to make myself.

CHAPTER 10: Page 230

The one in my family <u>who</u> does not want to become an American is my older brother. He does not accept the fact that it was necessary for us to come to this country. He was an engineer in Hungary, where <u>he</u> had a good position in a chemical factory. <u>It</u> was my father who insisted <u>on</u> our leaving because he could not bear the political situation. My brother was not interested in politic<u>s. He</u> made enough money to start saving for a car, which was his main interest in life besides his job. Now he cannot get a job here until he <u>has taken</u> more courses to improve his English and to pass an engineering test. In the meantime, he is working as a waiter and is very unhappy. He just wishes he <u>could</u> be back in Hungary. On the other hand, I like it here very muc<u>h, es</u>pecially because we have a larger apartment, and I share my room only with my brother instead of three people. Also, it is muc<u>h e</u>asier for me to meet other young peopl<u>e. I</u> can talk to anyone I want without worrying about his <u>political</u> beliefs.

Once I was walking with an American friend along the Bowery, when we saw two Chinese men walking with their arms around each other's neck.* My American friend insisted that those men were gay. I told him that he was wrong, explaining what I meant. According to Chinese custom, if two men are really good friends, they will often put their arms around each other. They consider this a sign of normal friendship. Chinese men are not afraid to show feeling for another man in public. My American friend said that although he understood, he would rather not put his arm around a friend's neck; it would be misinterpreted by his people. In the United States today, men have to be careful how they act with other men because unfortunately people are very concerned about homosexuality.

* Note another possible correction of the fragment: When we saw two Chinese men walking with their arms around each other's neck, my American friend insisted that those men were gay.

Index